T H E   B O O K   O F

FRENCH
Cooking

HILAIRE WALDEN

Photographed by
SIMON BUTCHER

Published by Salamander Books Limited
LONDON

Published by Salamander Books Limited
129-137 York Way, London N7 9LG, United Kingdom

9 8 7 6 5 4 3 2 1

ISBN 0-86101-803-6

Produced by ZEBU
Editor: Vicky Hanson
Art Director: Vicky Zentner
Photographer: Simon Butcher
Photographer's Assistant: Giles Stokoe
Home Economist: Justine Dickenson
Home Economist's Assistant: Liz Comben
Stylist: Shannon Beare
Colour separation: Classic Scan Pte. Ltd., Singapore
Printed in Belgium by Proost International Book Production

Notes:
All spoon measurements are level.
1 teaspoon = 5 ml spoon.
1 tablespoon = 15 ml spoon.

CONTENTS

INTRODUCTION

French cooking has two faces: that of haute cuisine and that of the home. Haute cuisine is to be found in restaurants throughout France and is emulated the world over. *The Book of French Cooking*, however, is devoted to the cooking found in people's homes - a cuisine that is richly varied and rooted in tradition. Recipes are passed down from one generation to the next, and early in life all children learn a simple love and respect for good food. Although times are changing, the vast majority of French people still eat the dishes they have always eaten, particularly in their homes. Even those affected by the pressures of modern life still appreciate good cooking and will often find time to prepare traditional dishes at weekends.

With today's tastes in mind, the best regional recipes from France's rich culinary heritage have been selected for this book. The selection includes the bistro stalwarts Leeks Vinaigrette and Croque Monsieur; rich, slow-cooked Boeuf Bourguignon and Coq au Vin; light and delicate Sole Meunière; sunshine-filled Ratatouille; and classic pâtisserie such as Tarte au Citron.

— FRENCH REGIONAL CUISINE —

French cuisine is strongly regional. With three very different coastlines, several neighbours and many changes of climate and terrain, it is inevitable that local produce, cooking styles, dishes and tastes will vary throughout the country. Simple soups and hearty casseroles feature in colder areas; in areas with lakes and streams, especially in mountainous regions, freshwater fish are popular; while along the coasts sea fish dominate local cuisine. In areas where the climate suits dairy farming, particularly northern France, butter is the fat most commonly used in cooking and many dishes feature cheese and cream; in the hotter, drier south, more suited to the growing of olive trees, dishes are prepared with olive oil. It is in the south, too, where garlic comes into its own - contrary to popular belief, garlic is not used everywhere in France.

In addition to these geographical areas, France is also divided into provinces. They officially disappeared years ago, but they are still known by their original names and each retains its own character, particularly in the style of its traditional cuisine.

BRITTANY
The rocky coastline of Brittany shelters huge stocks of shellfish such as lobsters, oysters, mussels, clams, scallops and langoustines. Mussels are traditionally cooked as Moules Marinière, or stuffed and grilled. Further out to sea, fishing boats catch sardines, brill, turbot and sea bass.

The interior of Brittany benefits from the benign, warming influence of the Gulf Stream, which makes it possible to grow early vegetables such as artichokes, shallots, baby carrots, cauliflowers, potatoes and garlic. Much of the produce is for canning, freezing or drying. The meat of the sheep that graze on the salt marshes, known as pré-salé lamb, has a unique flavour and is a popular delicacy.

Little of Brittany's milk goes into cheese-making (the only well known cheese is Saint-Paulin) but the south of the province yields Brittany's famous butter, which is often lightly salted, unlike in the rest of France. Crêpes and galettes, well-known Breton dishes, are traditionally made from locally grown buckwheat although sweet ones are now more commonly made from wheat flour.

NORMANDY
The long coastline of Normandy makes this region one of fine seafood - Dover sole is the prime catch, but the great variety also includes sardines, mackerel, tuna, bass, turbot, John Dory, mussels, oysters, lobsters, langoustines and crawfish.

On the lush pastures inland graze the cows which produce the region's superb dairy products: rich butter, cream and cheeses such as Camembert, Livarot, Pont l'Evêque and Neufchâtel. Apple orchards are a common sight and many of the apples go to make cider and Calvados (apple brandy) which feature in many local dishes. As in Brittany, the salt marshes produce delicious pré-salé lamb.

PARIS AND THE ILE DE FRANCE
It may be difficult to imagine that this area has a tradition of country cooking, but it was once studded with small villages and market gardens which supplied the rest of the country with vegetable produce. Crécy is still famed for carrots (the main ingredient in soupe de Crécy), the towns of Clamart and Saint-Germain are known for their peas and Argenteuil for its asparagus. The region also produces cauliflowers, potatoes, artichokes and onions, and mushrooms (champignons de Paris) have been cultivated in the caves and disused quarries around Paris for centuries.

South of Paris, vast expanses of wheat fields yield the flour that accounts for the reputation of Parisian bread and pâtisserie. Brie, the local cheese, can vary considerably in quality as it may be made either in large commercial creameries or on a small scale on a farm in one of the 'designated' areas, such as Brie de Meaux or Brie de Melun.

CHAMPAGNE AND THE NORTH

Although the name of Champagne is often associated with sophistication, the traditional food is typical of other northern areas, with hearty soups, simple stews and dishes based on root vegetables and cabbage. Despite the production of Champagne, the local drink is more often beer than wine, and dishes are often cooked in beer, such as Carbonnade de Boeuf.

Along the coast, fish and shellfish go into many types of fish stew and around Dunkirk and Calais herrings and mackerel are the main catch. Herrings are served smoked and salted, often with a vinaigrette dressing and hot potato salad.

Although much of the region is now heavily industrialized, cereals, beet (for sugar) and hops (for brewing beer) are grown, and market gardening is an important activity. Vegetables such as cabbage, carrots, leeks, onions and potatoes are an important part of the diet. On the flat plains, wheat is grown for the important flour milling industry. Locally produced cheeses, such as the orange-rinded Maroilles, are often strongly flavoured and are traditionally eaten with a glass of beer as an accompaniment.

A dish rich in flavour, Cassoulet is a classic example of the cooking of Gascony. There are many versions, but all feature the local ingredients of duck or goose, sausages, garlic and beans.

ALSACE-LORRAINE

Because of their position on the Franco-German border and time spent under the rule of both countries, the cooking of the two north-eastern provinces of Alsace and Lorraine exhibits strong similarities to that of Germany. Cold winters also make for hearty, German-style dishes. There is a preponderance of pork, ham, sausages and choucroute (similar to German sauerkraut), often accompanied by horseradish and mustard. The Alsace city of Strasbourg is an important producer of foie gras.

As the climate is cold and damp, vegetables are limited to cabbage, Brussels sprouts and root vegetables. Tarts and pies, such as the classic Quiche Lorraine, have always been popular, as are sweet tarts made from fruits such as cherries from the sheltered valleys of Lorraine. Among the large range of popular cakes are Madeleines, originally from Lorraine. Local cheeses, such as Munster, are strongly flavoured and pungent.

FRANCHE-COMTE AND THE ALPS

This is a beautiful area of peaks and valleys, lakes and streams. The lakes and rivers are celebrated for trout, Arctic char, grayling, pike and crayfish; game is found in the mountains; and wild mushrooms in the woods and pastures. As in other mountain areas, hams and sausages are dried in the clear, crisp mountain air. In the valleys grow fine fruits such as peaches and apricots.

The dairy products of this area are exceptional, flavoured by the aromatic plants in the cattle pastures. The principal cheeses are Gruyère and Emmental (although both originally from Switzerland) as well as Beaufort, Reblochon and Tomme de Savoie, many of which feature in local dishes such as Gratin Savoyarde. In the south of the province, Dauphiné is France's largest producer of walnuts. Due to its proximity to both Provence and the Alps, Dauphiné cuisine features olive oil as well as butter and cream.

BURGUNDY AND LYONNAIS

With the best available natural resources to maintain its gastronomic reputation, the cooking of Burgundy is rich and varied. Large Charolais cattle provide lean meat that is ideally suited to the long, slow braising of dishes such as Boeuf Bourguignon, Bresse produces the famed poulet de Bresse, while the local countryside provides game, mushrooms, snails and river fish such as trout.

The key ingredient in Burgundian cooking is wine. White wine goes into the region's fish stews and ham and chicken dishes. Red wine is used in nearly all meat and game dishes, and in some poultry ones, such as Coq au Vin. The selection of cheese is wide, although only a few, such as Epoisses and Charolles, are well known, as they are usually produced on a small scale for local consumption.

Traditionally known as the 'temple of gastronomy', Lyon is the centre of an enormous charcuterie industry, with a range of products exported nationally and internationally. Onions are often used in Lyonnais dishes and are believed to be a hallmark of local cooking. The Lyonnais also have a love of chocolate, first encouraged by confiseurs who arrived from Italy in the 18th century.

PROVENCE AND LANGUEDOC-ROUSSILLON

The food of these Mediterranean provinces is colourful and richly aromatic, heady with garlic and olive oil and fragrant with herbs. Fish specific to the Mediterranean feature strongly in local cooking; anchovies for example, form the basis of Tapénade and Anchoïade. Of the larger fish, the commonest are sardines, sea bream, red mullet and sea bass, all of which are frequently charcoal-grilled or barbecued.

Almost every variety of sun-loving fruit and vegetable are grown. Flavourful tomatoes, aubergines (eggplant), courgettes (zucchini) and peppers (capsicum) make dishes such as Ratatouille, slowly cooked until almost melted (one of the secrets of Provençal cooking). Local fruits include cherries, peaches, nectarines, melons, apricots, strawberries, figs and pears, sold fresh or preserved as jam or crystallized fruit. At the eastern end of the region an Italian influence can be detected in dishes such as Pissaladière - a pizza-like tart. Towards the Pyrenees, pork dishes and pork products become more common, and a Spanish influence is apparent.

THE PYRENEES

On the western coast of this province lies the Basque country. Flame red is the Basque colour - from their tiled roofs to their traditional berets - and it is also the colour of their cooking, which is dominated by tomatoes and peppers. Basque cuisine relies largely on fish such as tuna, swordfish, sardines and anchovies. Sea salt is used for preserving anchovies and cod, as well as the famed jambon de Bayonne.

The emphasis is on hearty, simple soups and stews, and from the days when meat was an expensive luxury, many dishes are based on cornmeal, similar to Italian polenta. At the eastern end of the Pyrenees, food is influenced by the Mediterranean.

GASCONY

The food of Gascony is simple and rich - goose, duck, pork and foie gras form the basis of the diet and appear in many soups and stews, of which the best known is Cassoulet. Goose or duck fat are used for cooking rather than butter or oil. Garlic (which some now believe has helped protect Gascons against the heart disease their diet could cause) is used generously, and cloves are used whole rather than chopped - when cooked gently and slowly, as in Chicken with Garlic, the flavour becomes mellow and mild. Many fruits grow in the area, and the plump, shiny black prunes of Agen are reputed to be the best in the world. Milk, butter and cheese used to be rare commodities; cattle were used solely for ploughing, and even goats' milk and cheese have become popular only in the last 25 years.

THE WEST

Bordeaux, the major city of the west, is better known for its wines than its food, which is generally quite plainly cooked to allow the wines to shine through. One renowned dish is steak, often entrecôte, served with Bordelaise sauce. Further north in Charente dairying is an important activity, carried out on lush pastures which yield excellent butter. Charente also produces the famed brandy, Cognac.

The presence of the rich Atlantic coastline is reflected in the number of fish dishes, many of which are served as first courses. Oysters, mussels and clams are farmed along the coast and the most popular fish are sole, sardines (sometimes eaten raw with sea salt and bread and butter), skate, grey mullet, sea bream, whiting and monkfish.

The climate is very favourable for spring vegetables and fruit. Orchards and hedgerows yield blackberries, plums, apples, pears, chestnuts and walnuts. Perigord, one of the best known culinary areas of France, has a worldwide reputation for foie gras and truffles, and the practice of using pigs to sniff out this rare underground fungus continues to this day.

THE CENTRE

The heart of this region is the Massif Central, a remote, rugged area where the cooking is simple and substantial, designed to provide warmth and energy at little cost. Staple foods are root vegetables, cabbage and bread. Chestnuts, wild mushrooms, sausages, pork, ham and bacon feature strongly. On the slopes of the valleys that catch the summer sun, and in the provinces of Limousin and Bourbonnais, fruits are grown for pies, tarts and puddings such as Clafoutis.

The pride of the region is its cheeses, made from the milk of cows that graze on lush, herb-strewn pastures. The large variety includes Cantal and Saint-Nectaire as well as blue cheeses such as Bleu d'Auvergne.

THE LOIRE

This area has been known as the 'garden of France' for many years, and although the cooking is simple, the excellence of the produce lends it distinction. There are many market gardens that grow early vegetables such as artichokes, asparagus, carrots, salad leaves and potatoes. There are also abundant supplies of apples and pears, peaches, apricots, melons, strawberries and blackcurrants, often used in desserts and pâtisserie, especially fruit tarts such as Tarte Tatin. The area around Tours is famous for dishes made with prunes.

As the area is centred on a river and its tributaries, as well as being near the sea, fish is important. The Loire does not provide as much fish as it used to, but stocks are now building up again. Popular meats are poultry, pork and pork products such as rillettes. Cheeses are made from goats' milk and on a small scale - the best known are Sainte-Maure and Valençay. The local wines - red, white and sparkling, sweet and dry - are used to good effect in regional specialities such as Pork with Prunes, Peaches in White Wine and Salmon in Red Wine, an unusual combination that is successful because of the softness of the red wines.

VICHYSSOISE

45 g (1½ oz/3 tablespoons) butter
6 leeks, white parts only, sliced
300 g (10 oz) floury potatoes, diced
550 ml (20 fl oz/2½ cups) chicken or vegetable stock
300 ml (10 fl oz/1¼ cups) milk
70 ml (2½ fl oz/⅓ cup) double (thick) cream
salt and freshly ground black pepper
chopped fresh chives, to garnish

Heat the butter in a saucepan, add the leeks and potatoes and stir to coat with butter. Cover and cook gently, stirring occasionally, for 5 minutes, until beginning to soften.

Add stock and bring to the boil. Cover and simmer for 15-20 minutes, until the vegetables are tender.

Stir in milk then press mixture through a sieve. Leave to cool then stir in cream and salt and pepper. Cover and chill thoroughly, for at least 2 hours. Garnish with chives and serve in chilled bowls.

Serves 4.

Note: Floury potatoes such as King Edwards should be used to give the best texture.

WATERCRESS SOUP

25 g (1 oz/2 tablespoons) butter
1 onion, chopped
225 g (8 oz) potatoes, diced
550 ml (20 fl oz/2 ½ cups) chicken, veal or vegetable
    stock
2 bunches watercress, chopped
about 300 ml (10 fl oz/1 ¼ cups) milk
pinch of freshly grated nutmeg
salt and freshly ground black pepper
fresh chives, to garnish

Heat the butter in a saucepan, add the onion and cook gently, stirring occasionally, for 5 minutes, until soft. Add potatoes.

Stir in stock, bring to the boil and simmer for 15 minutes, until potatoes are tender. Add watercress and simmer for 30 seconds. Transfer to a blender or food processor and process very briefly (otherwise it will become 'gluey'). Press through a sieve and return soup to rinsed-out pan.

Stir in enough milk to give desired consistency. Add nutmeg and salt and pepper and reheat gently without boiling. Garnish with chives and serve.

Serves 4.

Note: For best results, use full-fat milk.

LENTIL SOUP

2 tablespoons olive oil
1 onion, chopped
2 cloves garlic, chopped
115 g (4 oz) thick-cut streaky bacon, diced
1 leek, sliced
2 carrots, diced
1 stick celery, sliced
175 g (6 oz/¾ cup) green or brown lentils
400 g (14 oz/1¾ cups) passata
4 tablespoons chopped fresh herbs such as parsley,
    tarragon, thyme and marjoram
1 bay leaf
salt and freshly ground black pepper
chopped fresh parsley and croûtons, to garnish

Heat the oil in a saucepan and cook the onion, garlic and bacon, stirring occasionally, for 4-5 minutes. Stir in vegetables, lentils, passata, chopped herbs, bay leaf and 850 ml (30 fl oz/3¾ cups) water.

Bring to the boil and simmer for 25 minutes, until vegetables and lentils are tender. Season, garnish with chopped parsley and croûtons and serve.

Serves 4.

-CREAMED CAULIFLOWER SOUP-

1 cauliflower, divided into flowerets
6 spring onions, cut into 2.5 cm (1 in) lengths
1 bay leaf
75 g (3 oz/ ¾ cup) flaked almonds
850 ml (30 fl oz/3 ¾ cups) vegetable, chicken or veal
   stock
250 ml (9 fl oz/1 cup) milk
salt and freshly ground black pepper

Cook cauliflower, spring onions, bay leaf and half the almonds in 550 ml (20 fl oz/2 ½ cups) of the stock for 10-15 minutes, until the cauliflower is tender.

Preheat grill. Spread remaining almonds in a single layer on a baking sheet and toast, turning occasionally, until lightly browned.

Remove bay leaf from soup and purée soup in a blender or food processor. Return to rinsed-out pan, add remaining stock, bring to the boil and boil for 3 minutes. Lower heat and stir in milk. Reheat gently without boiling and season with salt and pepper. Scatter with toasted almonds and serve.

Serves 4.

HERBED PEA SOUP

55 g (2 oz/¼ cup) unsalted butter
1 leek, finely chopped
1 small round lettuce, separated into leaves
about 850 ml (30 fl oz/3¾ cups) vegetable or chicken
    stock, or water
several sprigs of chervil
few sprigs of parsley
450 g (1 lb) fresh or frozen peas
salt and freshly ground black pepper
single (light) cream, to garnish

Heat butter in a saucepan, add leek and cook, stirring occasionally, for 5 minutes, until soft. Add lettuce and cook for 1-2 minutes, until leaves have wilted.

Add stock or water, chervil, parsley and fresh peas if using, bring to the boil and simmer for 10 minutes if using fresh peas. If using frozen peas, simmer for 5 minutes, until peas are tender.

Purée soup in a blender or food processor and return to rinsed-out pan. Add salt and pepper and reheat gently without boiling. If soup is too thick, add some boiling stock or water. Swirl in cream and serve.

Serves 4.

SOUPE DE CRÉCY

55 g (2 oz/¼ cup) butter
575 g (1¼ lb) small carrots, sliced
2 leeks, chopped
175 g (6 oz) floury potatoes, diced
leaves from 2 sprigs of tarragon, chopped
salt and freshly ground black pepper
tarragon leaves, to garnish

Heat 45 g (1½ oz/3 tablespoons) butter in a saucepan, add carrots and leeks and stir to coat with butter. Add potatoes, cover and cook over a gentle heat, stirring occasionally, for 5 minutes, until beginning to soften.

Add tarragon, 850 ml (30 fl oz/3¾ cups) boiling water and salt and pepper. Bring to the boil, cover and simmer for 25 minutes, until vegetables are very tender.

Allow soup to cool slightly then press through a sieve or purée in a blender or food processor. Return to rinsed-out pan and reheat gently without boiling. Add a knob of the remaining butter to each serving, garnish with tarragon leaves and serve.

Serves 4.

ONION SOUP

85 g (3 oz/ ⅓ cup) butter
700 g (1 ½ lb) large onions, thinly sliced
1 litre (35 fl oz/4 ½ cups) beef stock
300 ml (10 fl oz/1 ¼ cups) dry white wine
large pinch of mixed dried herbs
pinch of freshly grated nutmeg
salt and freshly ground black pepper
6 slices French bread
150 g (5 oz/1 ¼ cups) grated Gruyère cheese
flat-leaf parsley sprigs, to garnish

Heat the butter in a large, heavy saucepan, add the onions, stir to coat with the butter and lay a piece of greaseproof paper on top.

Cook over a very gentle heat, without stirring, for 20-30 minutes, until onions are soft and rich golden brown. Add stock, wine, dried herbs, nutmeg and salt and pepper and bring to the boil. Cover and simmer gently for 45 minutes. Meanwhile, preheat oven to 180C (350F/Gas 4). Arrange bread slices on a baking sheet and bake for 10-15 minutes, until dried but not browned.

Preheat grill. Divide soup among heatproof soup bowls. Float a slice of bread on top and sprinkle with cheese. Grill until cheese is bubbling and golden. Garnish with flat-leaf parsley sprigs and serve immediately.

Serves 6.

SOUPE AU PISTOU

115 g (4 oz/ ½ cup) haricot beans, soaked overnight
1 onion, finely chopped
150 g (5 oz) pumpkin, chopped (optional)
1 stick celery, sliced
2 small leeks, chopped
115 g (4 oz) baby turnips, diced
175 g (6 oz) small green beans, cut into short lengths
150 g (5 oz) shelled broad beans
3 ripe tomatoes, peeled and chopped
55 g (2 oz) fine vermicelli
salt and freshly ground black pepper
PISTOU:
handful of basil leaves
3 cloves garlic
6 tablespoons olive oil
75 g (3 oz/ ¾ cup) grated Parmesan cheese

Drain haricot beans. Put in a large saucepan with onion, pumpkin, if using, and 1.7 litres (60 fl oz/7 ½ cups) water. Bring to the boil and boil rapidly for 10 minutes. Cover and simmer for 1 hour. Add celery, leeks and turnips and cook for 10-15 minutes. Add remaining ingredients. Cook for 10 minutes until the beans and vegetables are tender.

Meanwhile, make the pistou. Coarsely chop the basil. Using a pestle and mortar, pound the garlic with the basil, then gradually add the oil, stirring until well blended. Stir in Parmesan cheese and 1-2 tablespoons of hot soup. Pour the soup into warmed bowls, spoon a little pistou into each serving, garnish with Parmesan shavings and serve.

Serves 6.

LEEKS VINAIGRETTE

12 small leeks
1½ tablespoons chopped fresh parsley
1 hard-boiled egg, chopped
dill sprigs and red pepper (capsicum) strips, to
    garnish
VINAIGRETTE:
1 tablespoon white wine vinegar
½ teaspoon Dijon mustard
salt and freshly ground black pepper
4-5 tablespoons olive oil

Arrange leeks in a steamer, cover and steam for 6-10 minutes, until tender. Drain on kitchen paper.

To make vinaigrette, whisk together vinegar, mustard and salt and pepper. Slowly add oil, whisking constantly. Transfer leeks to serving plates, pour over vinaigrette and leave to cool slightly. Sprinkle over chopped parsley and egg, garnish with dill sprigs and red pepper (capsicum) strips and serve.

Serves 4.

—MUSHROOMS À LA GRECQUE—

2 tablespoons olive oil
1 onion, finely chopped
1 clove garlic, chopped
1 tablespoon coriander seeds
300 ml (10 fl oz/1¼ cups) red wine
1 tablespoon tomato purée (paste)
bouquet garni
450 g (1 lb) button mushrooms
575 g (1¼ lb) ripe tomatoes, peeled, seeded and
    chopped
salt and freshly ground black pepper
flat-leaf parsley sprigs, to garnish

Heat oil in a large frying pan, add the onion
and garlic and cook, stirring occasionally, for
7 minutes, until beginning to colour.

Stir in coriander seeds, wine, tomato purée
(paste) and bouquet garni. Add mushrooms,
tomatoes and salt and pepper.

Bring to the boil then simmer for 10 minutes,
until mushrooms are just tender. Transfer to
a bowl and leave to cool. Cover and chill for
several hours. Remove bouquet garni.
Garnish with flat-leaf parsley and serve.

Serves 4.

Note: A bouquet garni is a bunch of fresh
herbs used to flavour a dish but removed
before serving. The herbs may vary but it
always includes parsley, thyme and a bay leaf.

CELERIAC RÉMOULADE

150 ml (5 fl oz/ ⅔ cup) mayonnaise
2-3 teaspoons Dijon mustard
1 teaspoon lemon juice
salt and freshly ground black pepper
450 g (1 lb) celeriac
2 tablespoons chopped fresh chervil or parsley

Put mayonnaise in a large bowl, add mustard and lemon juice to taste and season with salt and pepper. Peel and coarsely grate celeriac.

Add celeriac to a large saucepan of boiling water and cook for 30-60 seconds. Drain celeriac and rinse under cold running water. Drain again and dry on kitchen paper.

Mix celeriac into mayonnaise. Sprinkle with chervil or parsley and serve.

Serves 4.

Note: Celeriac tastes better if briefly blanched in this way, but it can also be eaten raw.

——RED PEPPER VINAIGRETTE——

4 red peppers (capsicum)
4 hard-boiled eggs, halved
50 g (2 oz) can anchovies in olive oil, drained
2 tablespoons capers
2 tablespoons chopped fresh flat-leaf parsley
VINAIGRETTE:
2½ tablespoons red wine vinegar
115 ml (4 fl oz/½ cup) olive oil
salt and freshly ground black pepper

Preheat grill. Place whole peppers (capsicum) on grill rack and grill, turning occasionally, until charred and blistered all over.

Leave until cool enough to handle then peel, working over a bowl to catch the juices. Cut in half and discard cores and seeds. Arrange pepper (capsicum) halves on serving plates and pour over juices from bowl.

To make vinaigrette, whisk together vinegar, oil and salt and pepper and pour over peppers (capsicum). Remove egg yolks from whites. Chop egg whites and scatter over peppers (capsicums). Arrange anchovies on top and sprinkle over capers. Sieve egg yolks over peppers (capsicum), sprinkle with chopped flat-leaf parsley and serve.

Serves 4.

TAPÉNADE

200 g (7 oz) small black olives, pitted
55 g (2 oz) capers
4 anchovy fillets
1-2 cloves garlic, crushed
1 tablespoon Dijon mustard
115 ml (4 fl oz/½ cup) olive oil
1 teaspoon chopped fresh thyme
½-1 teaspoon lemon juice
freshly ground black pepper
8 slices French bread
chopped fresh chives, to garnish

Using a pestle and mortar, pound olives, capers, anchovies, garlic and mustard to a smooth paste.

Work in a little oil, a drop at a time, then gradually add the remaining oil, pounding constantly. Stir in thyme, lemon juice and pepper to taste. If necessary, adjust the consistency by adding more oil (it should be a thick, spreadable paste).

Toast the bread on both sides. Spread with tapénade, garnish with chopped chives and serve.

Serves 4-6.

Note: Tapénade can be kept in a covered container in the refrigerator for several weeks. Serve at room temperature.

ANCHOÏADE

2 cloves garlic, crushed
2 x 50 g (2 oz) cans anchovies in olive oil, drained
1 ½ tablespoons chopped fresh basil
70 ml (2 ½ fl oz/⅓ cup) olive oil
2-3 teaspoons red wine vinegar
2 teaspoons tomato purée (paste)
freshly ground black pepper

Using a pestle and mortar, pound garlic and anchovies to form a smooth paste.

Pound in basil. Work in a little oil, a drop at a time, then gradually add the remaining oil, pounding constantly.

Stir in vinegar and tomato purée (paste) and season with pepper. Serve with crudités and country bread.

Serves 4-6.

Note: Anchoïade can be stored in the refrigerator in a glass jar. Stir and adjust the level of vinegar and basil to taste before serving.

─ SOFT CHEESE WITH HERBS ─

225 g (8 oz/1 cup) well drained fromage blanc,
  or medium-fat soft cheese
1 tablespoon chopped fresh parsley
1 tablespoon chopped fresh chives
1 tablespoon finely chopped shallot
1 tablespoon olive oil
2 tablespoons dry white wine
1 teaspoon white wine vinegar (optional)
salt and freshly ground black pepper
4 tablespoons crème fraîche or whipping cream
parsley sprigs and fresh chives, to garnish

Beat cheese for 2-3 minutes to lighten it. Beat
in parsley, chives, shallot, oil, wine, vinegar,
if using, and salt and pepper.

Lightly beat crème fraîche or cream and fold
into cheese mixture. Spoon into serving
bowl, cover and chill. Garnish with parsley
sprigs and chives and serve with crudités.

Serves 4.

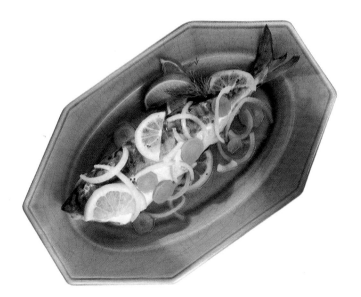

— MACKEREL IN WHITE WINE —

salt and freshly ground black pepper
6 small mackerel, cleaned and heads removed
1 lemon, sliced
1 small carrot, thinly sliced
1 onion, thinly sliced
½-1 fresh red chilli
12 coriander seeds
2 cloves
bouquet garni
70 ml (2½ fl oz/⅓ cup) white wine vinegar
about 300 ml (10 fl oz/1¼ cups) dry white wine
lime wedges and dill sprigs, to garnish

Season fish and lay it in a non-metallic flameproof dish. Cover with the lemon slices and vegetables, then add the spices. Add the bouquet garni and pour over vinegar and enough wine to just cover. Cover and leave to stand for 20 minutes.

Heat dish gently to simmering point. Immediately remove from heat and leave to cool. Discard chilli and bouquet garni. Arrange on serving plates, spoon over vegetables and juices, garnish with lime wedges and dill sprigs and serve.

Serves 6.

Note: The flavour of the mackerel will improve if kept in the refrigerator, covered, for a few days.

SAUTÉED CHICKEN LIVERS

55 g (2 oz / ¼ cup) unsalted butter
2 tablespoons finely chopped shallot
225 g (8 oz) chicken livers, trimmed
70 ml (2 ½ fl oz / ⅓ cup) dry white wine
115 g (4 oz) seedless green grapes, halved
salt and freshly ground black pepper
lemon juice (optional)
chopped fresh thyme or tarragon, to garnish

Heat butter in a large frying pan, add chopped shallot and cook, stirring occasionally, for 3 minutes, until soft.

Add chicken livers and cook quickly, stirring, for 1-1½ minutes, until crisp on outside and still pink in centre. Remove with a slotted spoon, cover and keep warm.

Stir wine into pan, dislodging sediment, and boil until slightly reduced. Lower heat, add grapes and heat gently to warm through. Return chicken livers to pan with any juices. Add salt and pepper and a squeeze of lemon juice, if necessary. Sprinkle with chopped thyme or tarragon and serve.

Serves 2.

——— PÂTÉ DE CAMPAGNE ———

350 g (12 oz) veal or chicken, finely chopped
700 g (1½ lb) fat belly pork, finely chopped
225 g (8 oz) calves' or lambs' liver, finely chopped
25 g (1 oz/2 tablespoons) butter
2 small onions, finely chopped
300 g (10 oz) streaky bacon, chopped
3-4 cloves garlic, finely chopped
2 tablespoons chopped fresh parsley
2 teaspoons herbes de Provence
2 teaspoons freshly ground black pepper
2 teaspoons salt
½ teaspoon ground allspice
115 ml (4 fl oz/½ cup) dry white wine
2 tablespoons brandy

Put veal or chicken, pork and liver into a bowl and mix well. Heat butter in a saucepan and cook onions, stirring occasionally, for 7 minutes, until lightly browned. Add onions to meats with all remaining ingredients and mix well. Cover and leave in a cool place for 2 hours. Preheat oven to 160C (325F/Gas 3).

Pack pâté mixture into a 1.65 litre (60 fl oz/ 7½ cup) terrine. Cover with foil. Put into a roasting tin and pour in enough boiling water to come three-quarters of the way up sides of terrine. Bake for 1½ hours. To test if cooked, insert a skewer in centre and count to 5. If skewer feels hot when withdrawn, the pâté is cooked. Remove from roasting tin and let cool. Put weights on top and chill for a few hours. Turn out, slice, and serve.

Serves 10-12.

PISSALADIÈRE

55 ml (2 fl oz/¼ cup) olive oil, plus extra for brushing
1 kg (2 lb) Spanish onions, thinly sliced
1 large clove garlic, crushed
salt and freshly ground black pepper
50 g (2 oz) can anchovies in olive oil
12 large pitted black olives, halved
1 teaspoon herbes de Provence
basil sprigs, to garnish
BASE:
225 g (8 oz/2 cups) strong white flour
1 teaspoon herbes de Provence
1 teaspoon easy-blend yeast

Heat oil in a large, heavy frying pan, add onions, garlic and salt and pepper and cook gently, stirring occasionally, for 25-30 minutes, until onions are well reduced, soft and golden. Leave to cool.

Meanwhile, make base. Stir together flour, herbs, yeast and salt and pepper. Slowly stir in about 175 ml (6 fl oz/¾ cup) tepid water to bind to a smooth dough.

Turn dough on to a lightly floured surface and knead well until firm and elastic. Lightly oil a 33 x 23 cm (13 x 9in) Swiss roll tin. Roll out dough to fit tin and use to line tin, pushing dough up sides and into corners.

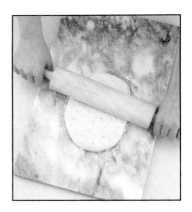

Brush with oil, cover and leave for 30 minutes until dough has risen and is lightly puffy. Preheat oven to 220C (425F/Gas 7).

Spread onions over dough. Drain anchovies, reserving oil. Cut anchovies lengthways in half and arrange in lattice pattern on top of onions. Arrange olives on top, sprinkle with herbs and drizzle over anchovy oil. Bake on top shelf of oven for 20-25 minutes. Cut into squares, garnish with basil sprigs and serve warm or cold.

Serves 4-6.

LEEK TART

55 g (2 oz/ ¼ cup) butter
4 leeks, halved lengthways and thinly sliced
salt and freshly ground black pepper
4 egg yolks
250 ml (9 fl oz/1 cup) milk or single (light) cream
leaves from 4 sprigs of tarragon, finely chopped
3 tablespoons freshly grated Parmesan cheese
   (optional)
PASTRY:
175 g (6 oz/1 ½ cups) plain flour
85 g (3 oz/ ⅓ cup) butter, diced
1 egg yolk

Heat butter in a large saucepan, add leeks and salt and pepper and cook over a low heat, stirring occasionally, for 10 minutes, until soft.

Leave leeks to cool. To make pastry, mix together flour and salt and pepper. Add butter and rub in until mixture resembles fine breadcrumbs. Stir in egg yolk and enough cold water to bind to a firm but not dry dough. Cover and chill for 30 minutes. Thinly roll out pastry on a lightly floured surface and line a 20 cm (8 in) flan tin. Prick base with a fork and line with foil or greaseproof paper. Fill with baking beans and chill for 20 minutes. Preheat oven to 200C (400F/Gas 6).

Bake pastry case for 10 minutes. Remove beans and foil or paper and bake for a further 10 minutes. Lower oven temperature to 180C (350F/Gas 4). Mix together egg yolks, milk or cream, tarragon, salt and pepper and Parmesan cheese, if using. Arrange leeks in pastry case and pour over egg mixture. Bake for 30-40 minutes, until lightly set and golden. Serve warm or cold.

Serves 4-6.

PAN BAGNAT

1 loaf French bread, cut into 4
1½ tablespoons white wine vinegar
1 teaspoon Dijon mustard
5 tablespoons olive oil
2 cloves garlic, crushed
salt and freshly ground black pepper
8 crisp lettuce leaves
4 ripe beef tomatoes, sliced
4 spring onions, thinly sliced
1 red pepper (capsicum), peeled (see page 25) and
   sliced
½ cucumber, sliced
12 basil leaves
16 pitted black olives
50 g (2 oz) can anchovies in olive oil, drained and
   coarsely chopped

Slice each piece of bread lengthways in half and pull out most of the soft bread from inside. Whisk together vinegar, mustard, oil, garlic and salt and pepper. Brush a little over inside of pieces of bread.

Cover bottom halves of bread with half the lettuce. Arrange tomatoes, spring onions, pepper (capsicum), cucumber, basil, olives and anchovies on top. Drizzle over remaining dressing, add remaining lettuce and cover with the top halves of bread. Cover with a board, put heavy weights on top and set aside for 2 hours. Cut each piece in half, garnish with basil sprigs and black olives and serve.

Serves 4.

CROQUE MONSIEUR

8 slices firm white bread
unsalted butter for spreading
115 g (4 oz/1 cup) grated Gruyère cheese
4 slices cooked ham
Dijon mustard for spreading
salad leaves and parsley sprigs, to garnish

Preheat grill. Butter one side of each slice of bread. Sprinkle half the cheese over buttered side of four slices, top with a slice of ham and spread with a little mustard.

Cover ham with remaining cheese, then put remaining bread on top, buttered side down, and press together. Grill sandwiches on both sides until bread is toasted and cheese melted. Cut in half, garnish with salad leaves and parsley sprigs and serve immediately.

Serves 2-4.

EGGS IN RED WINE

55 g (2 oz/ ¼ cup) butter, plus extra for spreading
115 g (4 oz) mushrooms, chopped
1 small onion, chopped
300 ml (10 fl oz/1 ¼ cups) red wine
175 ml (6 fl oz/ ¾ cup) vegetable or chicken stock
1 sprig of tarragon
4 eggs
salt and freshly ground black pepper
4 slices country bread, toasted
chopped fresh parsley and marjoram sprigs, to
    garnish

Heat half butter in a heavy saucepan. Add mushrooms and onion and cook gently, stirring occasionally, for 5 minutes, until soft.

Add wine, stock and tarragon. Bring to the boil and simmer for 10 minutes. Discard tarragon sprig. Remove vegetables with a slotted spoon and keep warm. Heat cooking liquid to just on simmering point. Carefully break in eggs and poach for 2-3 minutes. Remove with a slotted spoon, drain on kitchen paper and keep warm.

Boil liquid until slightly syrupy. Lower heat and whisk in remaining butter, a small piece at a time. Season with salt and pepper. Butter the toasted bread and top with vegetables. Place the eggs on top, pour over the sauce, garnish with parsley and marjoram and serve.

Serves 4.

Note: This dish can be made with white wine instead of red, if you prefer.

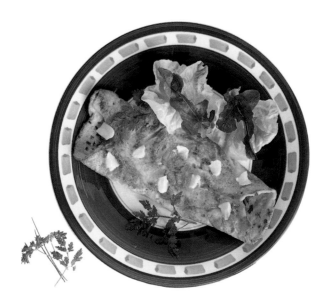

—— OMELETTE AUX HERBES ——

1 tablespoon mixed chopped fresh parsley, tarragon,
　chives and chervil
salt and freshly ground black pepper
3 eggs, very lightly beaten
25 g (1 oz/2 tablespoons) unsalted butter
chervil sprigs, to garnish

Add half herbs and salt and pepper to the
eggs. Heat half butter in a 23-25 cm (9-10 in)
frying pan. Pour the eggs into the frying pan
and cook over a moderate heat, stirring
gently with a fork or spatula and drawing egg
from the sides of the pan as it sets, to allow
the liquid egg to flow to the sides.

Stop stirring when egg is just set underneath
and still slightly liquid on top. Sprinkle with
remaining herbs and cook for 30-60 seconds.

Using a spatula or palette knife, flip over
one-third of omelette then flip over the other
side, to fold into three. Roll out of pan onto
a warmed plate. Dot with remaining butter,
garnish with chervil sprigs and serve.

Serves 1.

PIPÉRADE

4 thin slices Bayonne or Parma ham
1½ tablespoons olive oil
1 Spanish onion, chopped
2 cloves garlic, chopped
1 green pepper (capsicum), thinly sliced
1 red pepper (capsicum), thinly sliced
700 g (1½ lb) very ripe tomatoes, peeled, seeded and chopped
salt and freshly ground black pepper
6-8 eggs, beaten
parsley sprigs and chopped fresh parsley, to garnish

Trim fat from ham. Dice fat and heat with the oil in a heavy frying pan until the fat melts. Add onion and garlic.

Cook, stirring occasionally, for 5 minutes, until soft. Add green and red peppers (capsicum), tomatoes and salt and pepper and simmer gently for 15 minutes, stirring occasionally, until lightly thickened. Transfer two-thirds of vegetables to another pan, cover and keep warm. Put ham under a low grill to warm.

Stir eggs into remaining vegetables and cook over a low heat, stirring gently, until eggs begin to thicken. Immediately remove from heat. Put ham on warmed serving plates, top with vegetable mixture and then egg mixture. Garnish with parsley and serve immediately.

Serves 4.

GOUGÈRES

115 g (4 oz/ ½ cup) butter, diced, plus extra for
    greasing
150 g (5 oz/1 ¼ cups) plain flour, sifted
3-4 eggs, beaten
115 g (4 oz/1 cup) finely grated Emmental cheese
cayenne pepper
salt and freshly ground black pepper
beaten egg or milk for glazing
flat-leaf parsley sprigs, to garnish

Put butter in a saucepan with 225 ml (8 fl oz/
scant cup) of water and heat until melted,
then bring quickly to the boil. Remove from
heat and quickly stir in flour.

Return to a gentle heat and stir until mixture
comes away from sides of pan and looks
shiny. Remove from heat and stir for about
1 minute, until cooled, then gradually beat in
three-quarters of the beaten eggs, until
mixture is smooth. Add more egg as required
until mixture is glossy and soft, but not
runny. Beat in 85 g (3 oz/¾ cup) Emmental
cheese, cayenne pepper and salt and pepper.

Preheat oven to 200C (400F/Gas 6). Lightly
butter 2 baking sheets. Spoon mixture into a
piping bag fitted with a 1 cm (½ in) plain
nozzle. Pipe 48 small balls on to baking
sheets, spacing them 2.5 cm (1 in) apart.
Brush with beaten egg or milk, sprinkle with
remaining cheese and bake for 15 minutes
until well risen, crisp and golden. Garnish
with flat-leaf parsley and serve immediately.

Serves 6-8.

——MUSSELS WITH CREAM——

350 ml (12 fl oz/1½ cups) dry white wine
bouquet garni
2 kg (4 lb) mussels, scrubbed and trimmed
55 g (2 oz/¼ cup) butter
1 onion, chopped
½ teaspoon curry powder
1½ tablespoons plain flour
150 ml (5 fl oz/⅔ cup) crème fraîche or double
    (thick) cream
salt and freshly ground black pepper
flat-leaf parsley sprigs, to garnish

Put wine, bouquet garni and mussels in a
large saucepan and bring to the boil.

Cover tightly and cook over a high heat for
4 minutes, shaking pan occasionally, until
mussels open. Discard any mussels that
remain closed. Remove mussels from shells,
pouring their liquor back into pan and
discarding shells. Put mussels into a bowl,
cover and keep warm. Boil cooking liquid
until reduced by half.

Heat butter in a saucepan, add onion and
cook, stirring occasionally, for 5 minutes,
until soft. Add curry powder and flour and
cook, stirring, for 1½ minutes. Strain
cooking liquid and slowly stir into onion
mixture. Bring to boil, stirring, then simmer
for 4 minutes. Stir in crème fraîche or cream
and salt and pepper and boil until lightly
thickened. Stir in mussels, garnish with flat-
leaf parsley and serve.

Serves 4.

STUFFED MUSSELS

2 kg (4 lb) mussels, scrubbed and trimmed
3 sprigs of thyme
HERB BUTTER STUFFING:
1 shallot, finely chopped
2 cloves garlic, finely chopped
1 tablespoon finely chopped fresh parsley
1 tablespoon finely chopped fresh chives
1 teaspoon chopped fresh chervil
55 g (2 oz/1 cup) breadcrumbs made from stale bread
150 g (5 oz/⅔ cup) butter, softened
1-1½ tablespoons lemon juice
salt and freshly ground black pepper
flat-leaf parsley sprigs, to garnish

To make herb butter stuffing, mix together shallot, garlic, herbs and breadcrumbs then beat into butter. Add lemon juice and salt and pepper and set aside. Cover the base of shallow ovenproof serving dishes with a thick layer of coarse sea salt or crumpled foil. Pour 300 ml (10 fl oz/1¼ cups) water into a large saucepan. Bring to the boil, add mussels and thyme, cover tightly and cook over a high heat, for 4 minutes, shaking occasionally, until mussels open.

Preheat oven to 230C (450F/Gas 8). Drain mussels, discarding any that remain closed. Discard top shells of mussels and arrange mussels in dishes on top of salt or foil. Divide herb butter between mussels and bake for 10-12 minutes, until sizzling and golden. Garnish with flat-leaf parsley and serve at once.

Serves 4-6.

MOULES MARINIÈRE

25 g (1 oz/2 tablespoons) unsalted butter
2 shallots, finely chopped
2 cloves garlic, finely chopped
250 ml (9 fl oz/1 cup) dry white wine
bouquet garni, including parsley, thyme and chives
freshly ground black pepper
1 kg (2 lb) mussels, scrubbed and trimmed
3-4 tablespoons mixed chopped fresh herbs such as
   tarragon, chives, parsley and fennel
lemon juice (optional)

Heat the butter in a large saucepan, add the shallots and garlic and cook, stirring occasionally, for 2 minutes, until soft.

Add wine, bouquet garni and pepper and bring to the boil. Add mussels, cover tightly and cook over a high heat for 4 minutes, shaking the pan occasionally, until the mussels have opened. Discard any mussels that remain closed.

Remove mussels with a slotted spoon, transfer to large warmed bowls and keep warm. Discard bouquet garni. Add chopped herbs and lemon juice, if using, to cooking juices and simmer for 1 minute. Pour over mussels and serve.

Serves 2.

— MACKEREL & GOOSEBERRIES —

450 g (1 lb) gooseberries
1 teaspoon fennel seeds
2 x 450 g (1 lb) mackerel, each cut into 2 fillets
1 tablespoon olive oil
salt and freshly ground black pepper
1 tablespoon pastis
1 teaspoon sugar
25 g (1 oz/2 tablespoons) butter, diced
parsley sprigs, to garnish

Put gooseberries and fennel seeds in a saucepan with just enough water to cover. Bring to boil then simmer for 7-10 minutes, until very soft.

Meanwhile, preheat grill. With the point of a knife, make three slashes in each mackerel fillet. Season fish, brush with oil on each side and grill for 10 minutes, turning once.

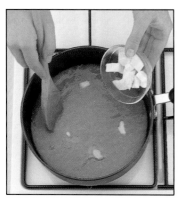

Reserve a few gooseberries for garnish. Press remainder through a nylon sieve into a saucepan, pressing hard to extract all the juice. Add pastis, sugar and salt and pepper and heat gently, gradually beating in butter. Pour sauce over fish, garnish with reserved gooseberries and parsley and serve with steamed vegetables.

Serves 4.

Note: Pastis is an aniseed-flavoured liqueur.

—SKATE WITH BROWN BUTTER—

85 g (3 oz/⅓ cup) unsalted butter
2 x 225 g (8 oz) skate wings
1 tablespoon chopped fresh parsley
salt and freshly ground black pepper
1 tablespoon lemon juice or white wine vinegar
2-3 teaspoons capers
lemon slices and flat-leaf parsley sprigs, to garnish

Gently melt butter in a small saucepan. Wring a piece of muslin out in very hot water, use to line a sieve and place over a jug. Pour butter through muslin, to remove white sediment. Pour about half of the clear butter into a large frying pan.

Add skate and cook for 4-5 minutes on each side. Drain on kitchen paper then transfer to warmed serving plates. Sprinkle with parsley and salt and pepper and keep warm.

Pour remaining clear butter into a small saucepan and heat until golden brown and nutty smelling. Add lemon juice or vinegar and capers and immediately remove from heat. Pour over skate, garnish with lemon slices and parsley and serve.

Serves 2.

——— HAKE WITH ORANGE ———

4 pieces of hake fillet, about 2.5 cm (1 in) thick
150 ml (5 fl oz/⅔ cup) milk
4 sprigs of tarragon
25 g (1 oz/2 tablespoons) butter, diced
salt and freshly ground black pepper
½ teaspoon finely grated orange rind
½ teaspoon finely chopped fresh tarragon
55 ml (2 fl oz/¼ cup) double (thick) cream
strips of orange rind, orange slices and tarragon
  sprigs, to garnish

Put fish in a single layer in a large frying pan. Pour over milk and lay a tarragon sprig on each piece of fish. Add butter and season with salt and pepper.

Cover with greaseproof paper and a lid, bring to simmering point, then lower heat and poach gently for 8-10 minutes, until flesh flakes easily.

Discard tarragon, transfer fish to warmed serving plates, cover and keep warm. Add orange rind and chopped tarragon to pan and boil for 2 minutes. Add cream and heat through, simmering for a few minutes if necessary, to thicken sauce. Pour over fish, garnish and serve.

Serves 4.

SOLE MEUNIÈRE

3 tablespoons plain flour
salt and freshly ground black pepper
8 x 75 g (3 oz) sole fillets
175 g (6 oz/¾ cup) unsalted butter
juice of 2 lemons
2 tablespoons finely chopped fresh parsley
parsley sprigs and lemon wedges, to garnish

Season flour with salt and pepper. Coat fish lightly and evenly in flour and set aside.

Gently heat 115 g (4 oz/½ cup) butter in a small saucepan until it foams. Wring a piece of muslin out in very hot water, use to line a sieve and place over a bowl. Carefully skim foam from surface of butter and pour butter through muslin, to remove white sediment.

Heat strained butter in a large frying pan until sizzling. Add fish, in batches, and cook over a moderate heat for 4 minutes on each side, until crisp but not brown. Transfer to warmed serving plates and keep warm. Pour off cooking juices and wipe pan. Add remaining butter to pan and heat until foaming and golden brown. Stir in lemon juice and parsley and immediately pour over fish. Garnish with parsley and lemon wedges and serve.

Serves 4.

— TROUT WITH ALMONDS —

salt and freshly ground black pepper
4 x 300 g (10 oz) trout, cleaned
70 g (2½ oz/⅓ cup) unsalted butter
50 g (2 oz/½ cup) flaked almonds
2 tablespoons lemon juice
dill sprigs and lemon wedges, to garnish

Season trout inside and out with salt and pepper. Heat 50 g (2 oz/¼ cup) of the butter in a large frying pan.

Add trout to pan and cook, in batches if necessary, for 12-15 minutes, turning once, until skin is crisp and flesh flakes easily. Drain trout on kitchen paper, transfer to warmed serving plates and keep warm.

Wipe pan with kitchen paper. Heat remaining butter in pan, add almonds and cook, turning occasionally, until lightly browned. Stir in lemon juice and salt and pepper. Quickly pour over fish, garnish with dill and lemon wedges and serve.

Serves 4.

──── TROUT IN RIESLING ────

55 g (2 oz/¼ cup) butter, diced
2 tablespoons finely chopped shallot
115 g (4 oz) mushrooms, sliced
4 x 300 g (10 oz) trout, cleaned
salt and freshly ground black pepper
300 ml (10 fl oz/1¼ cups) Riesling wine
115 ml (4 fl oz/½ cup) double (thick) cream
2 teaspoons finely chopped fresh parsley

Remove heads from trout, if preferred. Heat 40 g (1½ oz/3 tablespoons) of the butter in a frying pan large enough to hold fish in a single layer, add shallot and mushrooms and cook over a gentle heat, stirring occasionally, for 5 minutes, until soft. Lay fish on top and add salt and pepper and wine. Bring to just on simmering point, cover and poach fish for 10-15 minutes, until flesh flakes easily.

Transfer trout to warmed serving plates and keep warm. Boil cooking juices until reduced by half. Reduce heat, add cream and simmer until thickened slightly. Whisk remaining butter into the sauce, one piece at a time. Pour sauce over fish, sprinkle with chopped parsley and serve.

Serves 4.

—GRILLED BASS WITH FENNEL—

3 kg (6½ lb) bass or bream, cleaned and head
   removed
1 bunch of fennel
salt and freshly ground black pepper
juice of 1 lemon
3 tablespoons olive oil
lime slices and fennel sprigs, to garnish

With a sharp knife, cut deep diagonal slashes
in each side of fish and insert a fennel sprig
into each slash.

Preheat grill or barbecue. If using grill, line
grill pan with foil. Season fish inside and out
with salt and pepper and put 2-3 fennel sprigs
in cavity. Brush top half of fish with lemon
juice and oil and sprinkle a little lemon juice
and oil inside fish.

Put fish on grill or barbecue rack, lay a fennel
sprig on top and cook for 8-12 minutes, until
top half is cooked and skin is lightly charred.
Turn over carefully, brush with lemon juice
and oil and place another fennel sprig on top.
Cook for a further 8-12 minutes, until
cooked through. Cut into portions, garnish
with lime slices and fennel sprigs and serve.

Serves 6.

——— BARBECUED SARDINES ———

1 kg (2 lb) sardines, cleaned
6 tablespoons olive oil
3 tablespoons lemon juice
3 tablespoons mixed chopped fresh parsley, basil
   and tarragon
salt and freshly ground black pepper
basil sprigs, to garnish

Put sardines in a shallow non-metallic dish.
Mix together oil, lemon juice, herbs and salt
and pepper and pour over sardines. Cover
and leave in a cool place for 2 hours, turning
sardines occasionally.

Preheat grill or barbecue. Remove sardines
from marinade and grill for 2-3 minutes.
Turn over, brush with marinade and cook
for a further 3 minutes. Garnish with basil
sprigs and serve.

Serves 4.

STUFFED SARDINES

12 fresh sardines, cleaned and heads removed
1 clove garlic, finely chopped
1 tablespoon each chopped fresh chives, fennel,
    parsley and rosemary
1 tablespoon freshly grated Parmesan cheese
25 g (1 oz/¼ cup) almonds, lightly toasted and
    coarsely chopped
2 tablespoons olive oil, plus extra for greasing
salt and freshly ground black pepper
juice of ½ lemon
15 g (½ oz/¼ cup) fresh breadcrumbs
rosemary sprigs, to garnish

Preheat oven to 220C (425F/Gas 7). Oil a
wide, shallow roasting tin or ovenproof dish.

Open out sardines and lay, skin side up, on
work surface. Press gently with your thumbs
along centre of back to dislodge backbone.
Turn over and gently pull away backbone.

Mix together garlic, herbs, Parmesan cheese,
almonds, half the oil and salt and pepper.
Lay six sardines, skin side down, in a single
layer in roasting tin. Sprinkle with lemon
juice then spread with herb mixture. Cover
with remaining sardines, skin side up.
Sprinkle with breadcrumbs then drizzle over
remaining oil. Bake for 10 minutes until
golden. Garnish with rosemary sprigs and
serve hot or at room temperature.

Serves 6.

—SALMON WITH WATERCRESS—

unsalted butter for greasing
50 g (2 oz) shallots, finely chopped
4 x 200 g (7 oz) salmon fillets
salt and freshly ground black pepper
250 ml (9 fl oz/1 cup) dry white wine
250 ml (9 fl oz/1 cup) fish stock
4 bunches watercress
115 ml (4 fl oz/ ½ cup) double (thick) cream

Grease a frying pan large enough to hold fish in a single layer with a generous covering of butter. Add shallots, lay salmon on top, season with salt and pepper and pour over wine and stock.

Cover, bring to just on simmering point and poach gently for about 8 minutes, until fish is opaque and flesh flakes easily. Meanwhile, remove large stalks from watercress and discard. Add watercress to a pan of boiling water and blanch for 1 minute. Drain, rinse under cold running water and drain again. Purée in a blender or food processor.

Remove salmon from pan, transfer to warmed serving plates and keep warm. Boil cooking juices rapidly until thickened and reduced to 150 ml (5 fl oz/ ⅔ cup). Add cream and simmer until thickened to a coating consistency. Add watercress purée and heat gently to warm through. Pour sauce over salmon and serve.

Serves 4.

——SALMON IN RED WINE——

25 g (1 oz/2 tablespoons) unsalted butter
2 x 175 g (6 oz) salmon steaks
150 ml (5 fl oz/⅔ cup) soft red wine such as Chinon
    or Beaujolais
1 tablespoon chopped fresh tarragon
salt and freshly ground black pepper
tarragon sprigs, to garnish

Heat half butter in a frying pan, add salmon and cook each side briefly over a high heat.

Lower heat and cook salmon for 3 minutes on each side, until fish is opaque and flesh flakes easily.

Remove fish from pan, cover and keep warm. Stir wine into pan and boil until reduced by half. Add tarragon and salt and pepper. Dice remaining butter. Remove pan from heat and stir in remaining butter, one piece at a time. Divide sauce between warmed serving plates, place the salmon on top, garnish with tarragon sprigs and serve.

Serves 2.

—SCALLOPS IN WHITE WINE—

25 g (1 oz/2 tablespoons) unsalted butter
1 tablespoon olive oil
2 shallots, chopped
1 large clove garlic, crushed
115 ml (4 fl oz/ ½ cup) dry white wine
450 g (1 lb) shelled scallops
1 tablespoon lemon juice
2 tablespoons chopped fresh parsley
salt and freshly ground black pepper
flat-leaf parsley sprigs, to garnish

Heat butter and oil in a frying pan, add shallots and garlic and cook, stirring occasionally, for 5 minutes, until soft.

Add wine to pan and boil until reduced by about half. Cut each scallop into 2 or 3 slices, depending on size.

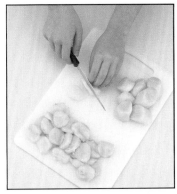

Add scallops to frying pan and cook, stirring occasionally, for 2-3 minutes until just turning opaque. Stir in lemon juice, parsley and salt and pepper. Garnish with flat-leaf parsley and serve immediately.

Serves 4.

Note: If the scallops still have their coral attached, you can use that too.

─ROAST GARLIC MONKFISH─

1 kg (2¼ lb) monkfish tail
1 head of garlic
2 tablespoons olive oil
½ teaspoon chopped fresh thyme
¼ teaspoon fennel seeds
salt and freshly ground black pepper
juice of 1 lemon
parsley and thyme sprigs, to garnish

Preheat oven to 220C (425F/Gas 7). Remove all fine skin from fish. Remove central bone then tie fish firmly back into shape with string. With point of a sharp knife, make a number of small incisions in fish.

Peel 2 garlic cloves and cut into slivers. Insert into incisions in fish. Heat half the oil in a frying pan, add fish and cook for 5 minutes, until evenly browned on both sides. Transfer to a shallow ovenproof dish and sprinkle with thyme, fennel seeds and salt and pepper.

Pour over lemon juice and remaining oil. Put remaining garlic, unpeeled, around fish and bake for 20 minutes. Garnish with parsley and thyme sprigs and serve with garlic cloves.

Serves 4.

Note: To eat garlic, squeeze flesh from skins and mash into cooking juices.

COQ AU VIN

25 g (1 oz/2 tablespoons) b
115 g (4 oz) thick-cut smo_____ y bacon, chopped
18 button onions
225 g (8 oz) button mu_
olive oil for frying (o_
6 chicken legs
1 onion, chopped
1 carrot, diced
2 cloves garlic
1 ½ tablespo_
550 ml (20 f_____ gundy wine
175 ml (6 f_____ tock
bouquet _
salt and _____ pepper
choppe _____ garnish

Heat _____ in a heavy flameproof casserole, add bacon and cook until crisp. Remove with a slotted spoon and drain on kitchen paper. Add button onions to casserole and cook, stirring occasionally, until golden. Remove with a slotted spoon and drain on kitchen paper. Add mushrooms to casserole, adding oil if necessary, and cook until lightly browned. Remove with a slotted spoon and drain on kitchen paper. Add chicken to casserole and cook over a moderately high heat until browned all over. Remove and drain on kitchen paper.

Add chopped onion and carrot to casserole and cook until lightly browned, adding garlic towards end. Sprinkle over flour and cook, stirring, for 2 minutes. Stir in wine and stock and bring to boil. Return all ingredients to casserole, add bouquet garni and salt and pepper, cover and cook very gently for 50-60 minutes. Remove chicken and vegetables, discard bouquet garni and boil sauce to thicken. Return chicken and vegetables to casserole. Garnish with parsley and serve.

Serves 6.

— CHICKEN WITH TARRAGON —

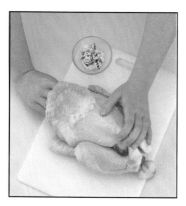

2 tablespoons finely chopped fresh tarragon
50 g (2 oz/¼ cup) butter, softened
1.5 kg (3½ lb) chicken
salt and freshly ground black pepper
115 ml (4 fl oz/½ cup) dry white wine
55 ml (2 fl oz/¼ cup) double (thick) cream
tarragon sprigs, to garnish

Preheat oven to 200C (400F/Gas 6). Beat tarragon into butter then push butter between chicken breast and skin.

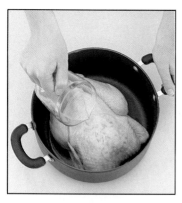

Season chicken with salt and pepper and put in a heavy flameproof casserole. Pour over wine. Cover tightly and cook in oven for 30 minutes. Lower oven temperature to 180C (350F/Gas 4) and cook for 1¼-1½ hours, until chicken is tender.

Transfer chicken to a warmed plate and keep warm. Tilt casserole and spoon off the fat, leaving behind cooking juices. Boil cooking juices to thicken to a light sauce. Reduce heat, stir in cream and simmer to thicken slightly. Carve the chicken, garnish with tarragon sprigs and serve with sauce.

Serves 4.

— CHICKEN WITH MUSHROOMS —

1 tablespoon olive oil
15 g (½ oz/1 tablespoon) unsalted butter, diced
4 chicken quarters
350 g (12 oz) chestnut, oyster, shiitake or chanterelle
   mushrooms, or a mixture
1 onion, finely chopped
175 ml (6 fl oz/¾ cup) Vouvray or similar fruity,
   medium-dry white wine
2 tablespoons chopped fresh tarragon leaves
115 ml (4 fl oz/½ cup) Greek or thick yogurt
salt and freshly ground black pepper
tarragon sprigs, to garnish

Heat oil and butter in a heavy flameproof casserole, add chicken and cook until browned. Remove with a slotted spoon.

Preheat oven to 160C (325F/Gas 3). Cut large mushrooms into quarters and oyster mushrooms into 2.5 cm (1 in) strips. Add to casserole with onion and cook, stirring occasionally, for 5 minutes, until soft. Stir in wine and bring to the boil. Return chicken to casserole and scatter over tarragon. Cover tightly and cook in the oven for 1 hour.

Using a slotted spoon, transfer chicken and vegetables to a warmed plate and keep warm. Boil cooking liquid to thicken slightly. Stir in yogurt and reheat gently without boiling. Season with salt and pepper. Return chicken and vegetables to casserole, turn in sauce and heat gently to warm through. Garnish with tarragon sprigs and serve.

Serves 4.

— CHICKEN BLANQUETTE —

4 rashers thick-cut streaky bacon, diced
15 g (½ oz/1 tablespoon) butter
1 small onion, chopped
4 boneless chicken breasts
450 g (1 lb) celeriac, chopped
1 bay leaf
250 ml (9 fl oz/1 cup) dry white wine or chicken
   stock
150 ml (5 fl oz/⅔ cup) crème fraîche or double
   (thick) cream
salt and freshly ground black pepper

Heat a flameproof casserole, add bacon and dry-fry until fat runs. Remove with a slotted spoon and set aside.

Heat butter in casserole, add onion and cook, stirring occasionally, for 2-3 minutes. Add chicken and celeriac and cook, stirring occasionally and turning chicken once or twice, for 5 minutes. Add bacon, bay leaf, wine or stock, and enough water to cover. Bring to the boil, cover and simmer gently for 30 minutes, until chicken is tender.

Remove the chicken, bacon and vegetables with a slotted spoon, transfer to a warmed plate and keep warm. Boil cooking liquid to thicken slightly. Discard bay leaf, stir in crème fraîche or cream, return to the boil and simmer for 3-4 minutes. Return chicken, bacon and vegetables to casserole, season with salt and pepper and heat gently to warm through. Serve.

Serves 4.

———— BURGUNDY CHICKEN ————

25 g (1 oz/2 tablespoons) butter
4 chicken legs
1 shallot, finely chopped
2 tablespoons Marc de Bourgogne or brandy
250 ml (9 fl oz/1 cup) white Burgundy or other
  Chardonnay wine
2 sprigs of thyme
salt and freshly ground black pepper
175 g (8 oz) seedless green grapes, halved
4 tablespoons crème fraîche or double (thick) cream
flat-leaf parsley and thyme sprigs, to garnish

Heat butter in a heavy flameproof casserole,
add chicken and cook until browned all over.
Remove and drain on kitchen paper.

Add shallot to casserole and cook, stirring
occasionally, for 2-3 minutes, until soft.
Return chicken to casserole. Pour over marc
de Bourgogne or brandy and set alight.
When flames have died down, add wine,
thyme and salt and pepper.

Bring to the boil, cover and simmer very
gently, turning chicken two or three times,
for 50-60 minutes. Transfer chicken to
warmed serving plates and keep warm. Add
grapes to casserole and boil until sauce is
thickened slightly. Stir in crème fraîche or
cream and simmer to thicken slightly. Pour
over chicken, garnish with flat-leaf parsley
and thyme and serve.

Serves 4.

POULET PROVENÇAL

10 cloves garlic
1 tablespoon finely chopped fresh thyme
1 tablespoon finely chopped fresh marjoram
salt and freshly ground black pepper
1.5 kg (3½ lb) chicken, cut into eight
2 tablespoons lemon juice
55 ml (2 fl oz/¼ cup) olive oil
1 sprig of thyme
1 small sprig of rosemary
6 basil leaves, shredded
8 anchovy fillets, drained and chopped
4 beef tomatoes, peeled, seeded and chopped
150 ml (5 fl oz/⅔ cup) dry white wine
24 Niçoise olives
chopped fresh herbs and basil sprigs, to garnish

Crush two garlic cloves and mix with the chopped herbs and a small pinch of salt. Cut small incisions in chicken and insert a little herb mixture into each incision. Rub with lemon juice and pepper and leave in a cool place for 2 hours. Preheat oven to 160C (325F/Gas 3). Heat half the oil in a saucepan. Finely chop remaining garlic and add to pan with thyme, rosemary and basil. Cook, stirring occasionally, for 5 minutes. Stir in anchovy fillets, tomatoes, wine and pepper. Bring to the boil and simmer for 15 minutes.

Heat remaining oil in a heavy, flameproof casserole, add chicken and cook until browned all over. Pour over sauce, cover and cook in the oven for 45 minutes, turning chicken once or twice. Add olives and cook for 15 minutes. Garnish with mixed herbs and basil sprigs and serve.

Serves 4.

Note: Niçoise olives have a special flavour as they are marinated in oil and herbs. If they are not available, use plain black olives.

POULET BASQUAISE

3 red peppers (capsicum)
1.3 kg (3 lb) chicken, cut into eight
salt and freshly ground black pepper
3 tablespoons olive oil
2 onions, thinly sliced
3 cloves garlic, chopped
½ fresh red chilli, cored, seeded and chopped
4 ripe beef tomatoes, peeled, seeded and chopped
bouquet garni
115 g (4 oz) Bayonne or Parma ham, diced
115 ml (4 fl oz/½ cup) dry white wine
chopped fresh parsley, to garnish

Preheat grill. Grill peppers (capsicum), until charred and blistered all over.

Leave peppers (capsicum) until cool enough to handle, then peel. Halve, remove cores and seeds and cut flesh into strips. Season chicken with salt and pepper. Heat oil in a heavy flameproof casserole, add chicken and cook until browned all over. Remove with tongs or a slotted spoon, transfer to a large plate and set aside.

Add onions and garlic to casserole and cook, stirring occasionally, for 5 minutes, until soft. Stir in chilli, tomatoes and bouquet garni and simmer for 15 minutes. Stir in ham, wine and peppers (capsicum). Bring to the boil, add chicken and any juices on plate and season with pepper. Cover tightly and simmer gently for 50-60 minutes. Transfer chicken to warmed serving plates. Boil sauce to thicken, pour over chicken, garnish with chopped parsley and serve.

Serves 4.

LEMON CHICKEN

55 g (2 oz/¼ cup) butter
1.5 kg (3½ lb) chicken quarters
16 button onions
250 ml (9 fl oz/1 cup) chicken stock
250 ml (9 fl oz/1 cup) dry white wine
bouquet garni
salt and freshly ground black pepper
12 button mushrooms, quartered
2 large egg yolks, lightly beaten
juice of ½ lemon
chopped fresh parsley, to garnish

Heat butter in a heavy flameproof casserole, add chicken pieces and onions and cook for 10 minutes, until chicken is browned.

Remove onions with a slotted spoon and set aside. Add stock, wine, bouquet garni and salt and pepper. Bring to the boil, cover and simmer for 20 minutes. Return onions to casserole and cook for 20 minutes. Add mushrooms and cook for 10 minutes.

Using a slotted spoon, transfer chicken and vegetables to a warmed plate, cover and keep warm. Boil cooking liquid until reduced by one-third. Remove a ladleful of cooking liquid, allow to cool slightly, then stir into egg yolks. Reduce heat, stir egg yolk mixture into casserole and heat very gently, stirring, until slightly thickened: do not boil. Stir in lemon juice. Return chicken and vegetables to casserole and turn in sauce. Garnish with parsley and serve.

Serves 4.

——————— BRAISED CHICKEN ———————

1.5 kg (3½ lb) chicken
1 onion, halved
2 cloves
115 g (4 oz) streaky bacon, chopped (optional)
about 1 litre (35 fl oz/4½ cups) stock or water
bouquet garni
salt and freshly ground black pepper
4 sticks celery, quartered
4 carrots, quartered
4 small turnips, quartered
12 small leeks, halved
bay leaves, to garnish

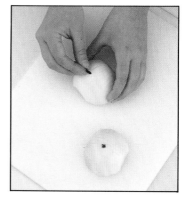

Put chicken into a large heavy flameproof casserole. Stud each onion half with 1 clove.

Add onion halves to casserole with bacon, if using. Add enough stock or water to cover and bring to the boil. Add bouquet garni and salt and pepper. Skim scum from surface, cover and simmer very gently for 1 hour.

Add celery, carrots and turnips, cover and cook for 30 minutes. Add leeks and cook for 15 minutes, until chicken and vegetables are tender. Transfer chicken and vegetables to a warmed serving plate and keep warm. Boil sauce to thicken slightly. Carve chicken and serve with the vegetables and sauce, garnished with bay leaves.

Serves 4.

CHICKEN CHASSEUR

1 tablespoon olive oil
45 g (1 ½ oz/3 tablespoons) butter
4 chicken quarters
3 shallots, finely chopped
1 clove garlic, finely chopped
1 tablespoon plain flour
150 g (5 oz) brown cap or shiitake mushrooms, sliced
250 ml (9 fl oz/1 cup) dry white wine
2 beef tomatoes, peeled, seeded and chopped
several sprigs of tarragon and parsley
salt and freshly ground black pepper
tarragon sprigs, to garnish

Heat oil and 30 g (1 oz/2 tablespoons) butter in a heavy flameproof casserole, add chicken and cook until browned all over.

Remove chicken and set aside. Add shallots and garlic to casserole and cook, stirring occasionally, for 5 minutes, until soft. Add flour and mushrooms and cook, stirring, until flour has browned lightly. Stir in wine and tomatoes. Bring to the boil, stirring.

Return chicken to casserole and add herbs and salt and pepper. Cover tightly and cook gently for 50-60 minutes. Remove chicken with a slotted spoon, transfer to warmed serving plates and keep warm. Remove herbs from sauce and discard. Boil sauce to thicken slightly. Lower heat and stir in remaining butter. Pour sauce over chicken, garnish with tarragon sprigs and serve.

Serves 4.

──POULET AU VINAIGRE──

1 tablespoon oil
15 g (½ oz/1 tablespoon) butter
4 chicken legs
1 onion, finely chopped
bouquet garni
4 ripe tomatoes, peeled, seeded and chopped
300 ml (10 fl oz/1¼ cups) red wine vinegar
2 teaspoons tomato purée (paste)
300 ml (10 fl oz/1¼ cups) chicken stock
salt and freshly ground black pepper
chopped fresh parsley, to garnish

Heat oil and butter in a heavy flameproof casserole. Add chicken and cook until lightly browned all over.

Remove chicken and set aside. Add onion to casserole and cook, stirring occasionally, for 5 minutes, until soft. Return chicken to casserole, add bouquet garni, cover and cook gently for 20 minutes, turning occasionally.

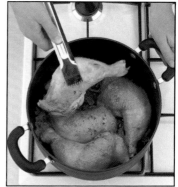

Add tomatoes to casserole, and cook, uncovered, until liquid has evaporated. Combine tomato purée (paste) and vinegar and add to casserole. Simmer until most of liquid has evaporated. Add stock and salt and pepper and simmer until reduced by half. Sprinkle with parsley and serve.

Serves 4.

GARLIC CHICKEN

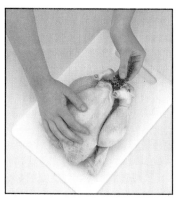

1 bunch of thyme
1.5 kg (3½ lb) chicken
2 heads of garlic, separated into cloves but not
    peeled
salt and freshly ground black pepper
175 ml (6 fl oz/¾ cup) dry white wine
15 g (½ oz/1 tablespoon) butter, diced
thyme sprigs, to garnish

Preheat oven to 200C (400F/Gas 6). Put some
thyme sprigs into cavity of chicken. Put
chicken into a heavy flameproof casserole
just large enough to hold chicken, and tuck
remaining thyme sprigs and a few cloves of
garlic around it.

Scatter over remaining garlic cloves, season
with salt and pepper and pour over wine.
Bring to the boil, cover tightly and cook in
the oven for 30 minutes. Lower oven
temperature to 180C (350F/Gas 4) and cook
for 1¼-1½ hours.

Transfer chicken and garlic to a warmed
serving plate and keep warm. Discard thyme.
Tilt casserole and spoon off fat, leaving
behind cooking juices. Boil cooking juices to
thicken slightly. Remove from heat and stir
in butter. Carve chicken, garnish with thyme
sprigs and serve with garlic cloves and sauce.

Serves 4.

Note: Garlic cooked in this way has a mild,
sweet flavour. To eat, squeeze cloves out of
skin and mash into sauce.

DUCK WITH ORANGE

2 x 175 g (6 oz) boneless duck breasts
salt and freshly ground black pepper
1 ½ teaspoons chopped fresh thyme
2 oranges
1 teaspoon cornflour
juice of 1 lemon
4 tablespoons Cointreau
15 g (½ oz/1 tablespoon) unsalted butter
orange twists and thyme sprigs, to garnish

Using a sharp knife, score skin and fat on duck breasts in a criss-cross pattern, taking care not to cut through flesh. Season with salt and pepper and rub with thyme.

Heat a heavy frying pan, add duck, skin side down, and cook over a moderate to high heat for 10-12 minutes, lowering heat a little if skin becomes too brown. Turn duck over and cook for 5 minutes, or to taste. Transfer duck to a warmed plate and keep warm.

Meanwhile, pare enough rind from oranges to give 1½ tablespoons. Add to a small pan of boiling water and blanch for 2 minutes. Drain, rinse in cold water and set aside. Squeeze juice from oranges. Pour most of fat from frying pan. Stir cornflour into pan then add orange and lemon juice and orange rind. Bring to the boil, stirring, then add Cointreau and salt and pepper. Reduce heat and whisk in butter. Slice duck, arrange on serving plates, pour over sauce, garnish and serve.

Serves 2.

DUCK WITH TURNIPS

1.8-2.3 kg (4-5 lb) duck
salt and freshly ground black pepper
1 tablespoon olive oil
250 ml (9 fl oz/1 cup) chicken stock
115 ml (4 fl oz/½ cup) dry white wine
bouquet garni
pinch of sugar
575 g (1¼ lb) small turnips, halved or quartered
sage sprigs, to garnish

Season duck generously inside and out with salt and pepper and prick fatty areas of breasts with a fork.

Heat oil in a heavy flameproof casserole, add duck and cook over a low heat, turning, until browned all over. Pour fat from casserole, reserving 2 tablespoons. Add stock, wine and bouquet garni to casserole, cover tightly and cook gently for 30 minutes.

Meanwhile, heat reserved duck fat in a frying pan, add turnips, sprinkle with sugar and cook until browned all over. Add turnips to casserole, baste with cooking liquid and cook, uncovered, for 25 minutes, until duck and turnips are tender. Transfer duck and turnips to a warmed serving plate. Skim fat from sauce then boil sauce to thicken slightly. Season with salt and pepper and remove bouquet garni. Carve duck, garnish and serve with turnips and sauce.

Serves 4.

BOEUF BOURGUIGNON

1-2 tablespoons olive oil
2 rashers thick-cut streaky bacon, chopped
12 each button onions and button mushrooms
1 kg (2 lb) braising steak, cubed
1 large onion, finely chopped
1 carrot, finely chopped
3 cloves garlic, chopped
1 tablespoon plain flour
685 ml (24 fl oz/3 cups) red Burgundy wine
bouquet garni
salt and freshly ground black pepper
chopped fresh parsley, parsley sprigs and bay leaves,
    to garnish

Heat 1 tablespoon oil in a heavy flameproof
casserole and cook bacon for 2-3 minutes.

Remove with a slotted spoon and set aside.
Add button onions to casserole and cook,
stirring occasionally, until browned. Remove
with a slotted spoon and set aside. Add
mushrooms to casserole and cook, stirring
occasionally, until lightly browned, adding
more oil if necessary. Remove with a slotted
spoon and set aside. Add beef to casserole
and cook over a moderately high heat until
browned all over. Remove with a slotted
spoon and set aside.

Add chopped onion and carrot to casserole
and cook, stirring occasionally, until
beginning to brown. Return bacon and beef
to casserole, add garlic and stir in flour. Stir
in wine, bouquet garni, salt and plenty of
pepper. Heat to almost simmering, cover and
cook very gently for 2¾ hours, stirring
occasionally. Add reserved onions and
mushrooms, cover and cook for 10 minutes,
to warm through. Garnish with parsley and
bay leaves and serve.

Serves 4.

– BOEUF EN DAUBE PROVENÇAL –

1 kg (2 ¼ lb) braising steak, cubed
1 Spanish onion, chopped
3 cloves garlic, chopped
bouquet garni
1 teaspoon black peppercorns
685 ml (24 fl oz/3 cups) full-bodied red wine
2 tablespoons olive oil
225 g (8 oz) streaky bacon, cut into strips
3 tomatoes, peeled, seeded and chopped
5 cm (2 in) wide strip of orange peel, oven-dried
salt and freshly ground black pepper
12 black olives
flat-leaf parsley sprigs, to garnish

Put steak, onion, garlic, bouquet garni, peppercorns and wine in a non-metallic bowl.

Cover and leave to marinate for 12-24 hours. Preheat oven to 160C (325F/Gas 3). Remove meat from marinade with a slotted spoon, reserving marinade, and drain beef on kitchen paper. Heat oil in a heavy flameproof casserole, add bacon and cook until browned. Remove with a slotted spoon and set aside. Add beef and cook over a moderately high heat until browned all over. Add tomatoes and cook for 2-3 minutes.

Add reserved marinade, bacon and orange peel and season with salt and pepper. Heat to almost simmering, cover tightly and cook in oven for 3 ¼ hours. Add olives and cook for 15 minutes. Discard bouquet garni and orange peel, garnish with parsley and serve.

Serves 4-6.

Note: To dry orange peel, put in a very low oven and leave until hard.

—— BEEF FILLET BORDELAISE ——

200 g (7 oz) bone marrow (optional)
50 g (2 oz/¼ cup) butter
50 g (2 oz) shallots, finely chopped
175 ml (6 fl oz/¾ cup) red Bordeaux wine
bouquet garni
1 tablespoon olive oil
450 g (1 lb) piece beef fillet
salt and freshly ground black pepper
1 tablespoon chopped fresh parsley

Put marrow, if using, in a saucepan, cover with water and bring to the boil. Remove from heat and set aside. Heat half butter in a saucepan, add shallots and cook, stirring occasionally, for 3-5 minutes, until soft.

Add wine and bouquet garni, bring to the boil and boil until reduced by half. Meanwhile, heat oil in a frying pan, add beef and fry for 2-4 minutes on each side, according to taste. Transfer to a warmed plate, season and keep warm. Remove bouquet garni from sauce and season sauce with salt and pepper. Reduce heat and whisk in remaining butter.

Cut beef diagonally into 4 thick slices. Drain marrow, cut diagonally into 4 slices and add to sauce. Pour sauce over beef, sprinkle with parsley and serve immediately.

Serves 2.

-STEAK WITH BÉARNAISE SAUCE-

olive oil for brushing
4 sirloin steaks, about 2.5 cm (1 in) thick
salt and freshly ground black pepper
BÉARNAISE SAUCE:
115 g (4 oz/ ½ cup) unsalted butter, diced
3 stalks each tarragon and chervil
2 teaspoons chopped shallot
4 black peppercorns, crushed
2 tablespoons dry white wine
2 tablespoons white wine vinegar
2 egg yolks
1 teaspoon each chopped fresh tarragon, parsley and
   chervil

Preheat grill. Oil grill rack, add steaks and
season with black pepper.

Grill for 1-3 minutes on each side, according
to taste. Meanwhile, make sauce. Melt butter
in a small saucepan then set aside and cool
slightly. Put tarragon and chervil stalks,
shallot, peppercorns, wine and vinegar in a
small saucepan, bring to the boil and boil
until reduced to 2 teaspoons. Strain.

Put egg yolks in a blender or food processor
with 2 teaspoons water and process briefly to
combine. With motor running at low speed,
pour in reduced liquid. With motor still
running at low speed, pour in melted butter
in a slow, steady stream, to make a thick
sauce. Add herbs and salt and pepper and
serve immediately with steaks.

Serves 4.

CARBONNADE DE BOEUF

2 tablespoons olive oil
1 kg (2 lb) braising steak, cubed
450 g (1 lb) onions, sliced
2 tablespoons plain flour
550 ml (20 fl oz/2½ cups) brown ale
1 clove garlic, crushed
bouquet garni
4 thick slices French bread
salt and freshly ground black pepper
Dijon mustard for spreading
flat-leaf parsley and chopped fresh parsley, to
    garnish.

Heat oil in a heavy flameproof casserole, add
meat and cook until browned all over.
Remove with a slotted spoon and set aside.

Add onions to casserole and cook gently,
stirring occasionally, for 10 minutes, until
browned. Sprinkle over flour and cook,
stirring, until lightly browned. Stir in beer
and bring to boil, stirring. Return beef to
casserole, add garlic and bouquet garni, cover
tightly and cook very gently for 2 hours,
stirring occasionally.

Preheat grill to low. Toast bread slowly until
crisp and golden. Spread thickly with
mustard, baste lightly with sauce from
casserole and toast for 5-10 minutes, until
topping is browned. Garnish casserole with
parsley and serve with mustard croûtes.

Serves 4.

NAVARIN OF LAMB

1 tablespoon olive oil
1 kg (2¼ lb) boneless lamb, cubed
1 onion and 1 large carrot, finely chopped
pinch of sugar
2 teaspoons plain flour
115 ml (4 fl oz/½ cup) dry white wine
550 ml (20 fl oz/2½ cups) veal or chicken stock
bouquet garni
salt and freshly ground black pepper
3 ripe tomatoes, peeled, seeded and chopped
3 small turnips, quartered
12 button onions
12 small new potatoes
12 baby carrots, halved or quartered
150 g (5 oz) shelled fresh peas or small broad beans
parsley sprigs, to garnish

Heat oil in a heavy flameproof casserole, add lamb and cook until browned all over. Remove with a slotted spoon and set aside. Add chopped onion and carrot and cook, stirring occasionally, for 10 minutes, until browned. Sprinkle over sugar and flour and cook, stirring, until lightly browned. Add wine, stock, bouquet garni and salt and pepper. Add tomatoes and bring to the boil, stirring. Return lamb to casserole, cover tightly and cook gently for 30 minutes.

Add turnips, onions and potatoes, cover and cook for 20 minutes. Add carrots and cook for 10 minutes. Add peas or beans and cook for 5-7 minutes. Remove meat and vegetables with a slotted spoon, transfer to a warmed plate and keep warm. Boil cooking juices to thicken slightly. Return lamb and vegetables to casserole and turn in sauce. Garnish with parsley and serve.

Serves 4.

LAMB BOULANGÈRE

2 kg (4½ lb) leg of lamb
4 cloves garlic
salt and freshly ground black pepper
1 kg (2 lb) potatoes, fairly thickly sliced
1 Spanish onion, thinly sliced
1 bay leaf
2 sprigs of thyme
about 300 ml (10 fl oz/1¼ cups) veal or vegetable
  stock or water
40 g (1½ oz/3 tablespoons) butter
olive oil for greasing
salt and freshly ground black pepper
flat-leaf parsley, to garnish

Cut small incisions in lamb. Thinly slice two
garlic cloves and insert into incisions.

Season lamb and set aside. Preheat oven
to 160C (325F/Gas 3). Grease a shallow
ovenproof dish with 15 g (½ oz/1 tablespoon)
butter. Crush remaining garlic. Arrange
layers of potatoes, onion, garlic, herbs and
salt and pepper in the buttered dish. Add
enough stock or water to just cover, dot with
remaining butter, cover with foil and bake in
the oven for 1 hour.

Grease a heavy frying pan with a little oil,
add lamb and cook quickly until lightly
browned all over. Put lamb on top of
potatoes and cover with foil. Increase oven
temperature to 190C (375F/Gas 5) and bake
lamb and potatoes for 1¼-1½ hours,
uncovering 15 minutes before end of cooking
time, to brown. Carve lamb, garnish with
flat-leaf parsley and serve with potatoes.

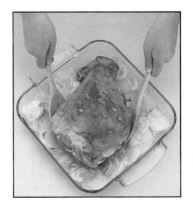

Serves 6.

—LAMB & FLAGEOLET BEANS—

4 x 225 g (8 oz) lamb shanks
4 cloves garlic, thinly sliced
2 tablespoons olive oil
1 onion, finely chopped
350 g (12 oz/1 ½ cups) flageolet beans, soaked
  overnight
575 g (1 ¼ lb) tomatoes, peeled, seeded and chopped
1 tablespoon tomato purée (paste)
150 ml (5 fl oz/⅔ cup) red wine
bouquet garni
salt and freshly ground black pepper
1 small bunch of parsley, chopped
flat-leaf parsley and bay leaves, to garnish

Cut 4 incisions in each lamb shank. Insert a slice of garlic in each incision.

Heat oil in a heavy flameproof casserole, add shanks and cook until browned all over. Remove and set aside. Add onion and remaining garlic to casserole and cook, stirring occasionally, for 5 minutes, until soft but not browned.

Drain and rinse beans and add to casserole with tomatoes, tomato purée (paste), wine, bouquet garni and salt and pepper. Return lamb to casserole, cover tightly and cook gently for 1-2 hours, until lamb and flageolet beans are tender. Discard bouquet garni and stir in parsley. Garnish and serve with béarnaise sauce (see page 74).

Serves 4.

——— LAMB WITH ROSEMARY ———

2 kg (4 ½ lb) leg of young lamb
3 sprigs of rosemary
2-3 cloves garlic, cut into slivers
salt and freshly ground black pepper
50 g (2 oz/¼ cup) butter
150 ml (5 fl oz/⅔ cup) red or white wine

Preheat oven to 230C (450F/Gas 8). Cut small incisions in lamb with the point of a sharp knife.

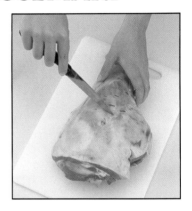

Remove leaves from one rosemary sprig. Insert leaves and garlic slivers into incisions. Season lamb, put the remaining rosemary sprigs on top and dot with butter. Put in a roasting tin and roast for 15 minutes. Lower oven temperature to 180C (350F/Gas 4) and roast for a further 40-60 minutes.

Leave lamb in oven, with door propped open, for 15 minutes, to rest. Remove lamb from roasting tin and transfer to a serving plate. Tilt roasting tin and spoon off most of fat. Add wine, stirring to dislodge sediment. Bring to the boil and simmer briefly. Season with salt and pepper. Carve lamb, garnish with rosemary sprigs and serve with sauce.

Serves 6.

— TARRAGON LAMB NOISETTES —

1 tablespoon olive oil
50 g (2 oz/¼ cup) butter
8 lamb noisettes, about 2.5 cm (1 in) thick
salt and freshly ground black pepper
4 tablespoons brandy
3 tablespoons double (thick) cream
2 tablespoons chopped fresh tarragon
tarragon sprigs and flat-leaf parsley, to garnish

Heat oil and half the butter in a heavy frying pan until sizzling.

Add lamb and cook for 2½-3 minutes on each side, until well-browned but still pink in the centre. Remove with a slotted spoon, transfer to warmed serving plates, season with salt and pepper and keep warm.

Add remaining butter to pan. When melted, add brandy, stirring to dislodge sediment, and bring to the boil. Stir in cream and tarragon and boil until thickened. Season, pour over lamb, garnish with tarragon sprigs and flat-leaf parsley and serve.

Serves 4.

KIDNEYS IN RED WINE

45 g (1 ½ oz/3 tablespoons) butter
3 shallots, finely chopped
1 clove garlic, finely chopped
115 ml (4 fl oz/ ½ cup) red wine
bouquet garni
salt and freshly ground black pepper
1 tablespoon olive oil
450 g (1 lb) lambs' kidneys, halved and cored
2 teaspoons Dijon mustard
2 tablespoons double (thick) cream
salt and freshly ground black pepper
flat-leaf parsley and chopped parsley, to garnish

Heat 25 g (1 oz/2 tablespoons) butter in a
saucepan, add shallots and garlic and cook,
stirring occasionally, for 3 minutes, until soft.

Add wine, 3 tablespoons water, bouquet
garni and salt and pepper. Bring to the boil
and simmer for 5 minutes. Discard bouquet
garni. Meanwhile, heat oil and remaining
butter in a large frying pan, add kidneys and
cook, stirring, over a moderately high heat
for 3-4 minutes. Remove with a slotted
spoon and keep warm.

Stir wine sauce, mustard and cream into pan,
stirring to dislodge sediment. Add kidneys,
together with any juices on plate, and heat
through gently: do not boil. Garnish with
parsley and serve.

Serves 3-4.

——— RABBIT WITH MUSTARD ———

85 g (3 oz/⅓ cup) butter
1.5 kg (3½ lb) boneless rabbit portions
salt and freshly ground black pepper
olive oil for greasing
50 g (2 oz) Dijon mustard
50 g (2 oz/1 cup) fresh breadcrumbs
1 tablespoon chopped fresh tarragon
tarragon sprigs, to garnish

Heat 50 g (2 oz/4 tablespoons) butter in a frying pan. Add rabbit and cook until lightly browned all over.

Season with salt and pepper. Remove with a slotted spoon, transfer to a wire rack and leave for 10 minutes. Preheat oven to 240C (475F/Gas 9). Oil a roasting tin. Spread mustard over rabbit portions then coat in breadcrumbs. Put in roasting tin in a single layer and bake for 20 minutes.

Transfer rabbit portions to a warmed dish and keep warm. Melt remaining butter and pour over rabbit. Sprinkle with chopped tarragon, garnish with tarragon and serve.

Serves 4.

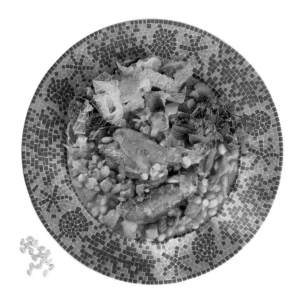

CASSOULET

350 g (12 oz/1 ½ cups) haricot beans, soaked overnight
2 tablespoons olive oil
175 g (6 oz) thick-cut smoked streaky bacon, chopped
6 coarse-cut pork sausages
3 duck leg portions, halved
2 large onions, chopped
2 cloves garlic, crushed
350 g (12 oz) ripe tomatoes, peeled and chopped
1 ½ tablespoons tomato purée (paste)
115 ml (4 fl oz/ ½ cup) dry white wine
large bunch of fresh herbs
salt and freshly ground black pepper
fresh herbs and chopped fresh parsley, to garnish

Drain and rinse beans. Put in a saucepan, cover with cold water and bring to the boil.

Boil rapidly for 10 minutes, reduce heat and simmer for 50 minutes, until just tender. Drain beans, reserving 250 ml (9 fl oz/1 cup) cooking liquid. Preheat oven to 160C (325F/ Gas 3). Heat oil in a large flameproof casserole, add bacon and sausages and cook until lightly browned. Remove with a slotted spoon and drain on kitchen paper. Add duck portions to casserole and cook until lightly browned. Remove with a slotted spoon and drain on kitchen paper.

Add onions to casserole and cook, stirring occasionally, for 7 minutes, until beginning to colour. Return meats to casserole with beans, reserved cooking liquid and remaining ingredients. Bring to the boil, cover and cook in oven for 1-1 ¼ hours, uncovering towards end of cooking to thicken juices. Garnish with herbs and parsley and serve.

Serves 6.

——MARINATED SPICED PORK——

1 tablespoon olive oil
1.5 kg (3½ lb) leg of pork, skin and fat removed
115 g (4 oz) brown cap or shiitake mushrooms, sliced
thyme sprigs and celery leaves, to garnish
MARINADE:
2 tablespoons olive oil
1 onion, finely chopped
1 carrot, finely chopped
1 stick celery, chopped
450 ml (16 fl oz/2 cups) full-bodied red wine
6 juniper berries, crushed
8 peppercorns, crushed
¼ teaspoon ground allspice
bouquet garni
salt

To make marinade, heat the oil in a heavy frying pan, add onion and carrot and cook, stirring occasionally, for 5 minutes. Add celery and cook, stirring occasionally, until vegetables are browned. Add wine, juniper berries, peppercorns, allspice, bouquet garni and salt. Leave to cool. Put pork in a non-metallic dish, pour over marinade, cover and leave in a cool place for 24 hours, turning pork occasionally. Preheat oven to 180C (350F/Gas 4). Remove pork and vegetables with a slotted spoon and drain pork on kitchen paper. Strain marinade and set aside.

Heat oil in a heavy flameproof casserole just large enough to hold pork, add pork and cook until browned all over. Remove and set aside. Add mushrooms and cook for 5 minutes. Add reserved vegetables and put pork on top. Pour over marinade. Heat to almost simmering, cover and cook in oven, turning occasionally, for 2-2½ hours. Transfer to a warmed plate. Skim excess fat from sauce then boil to thicken. Season. Carve pork, garnish and serve with sauce.

Serves 4-6.

PORK WITH PRUNES

150 g (5 oz) large prunes
550 ml (20 fl oz/2 ½ cups) dry white wine
45 g (1 ½ oz/3 tablespoons) butter
4 pork chops
225 g (8 oz) mixed chopped onion, carrot and celery
250 ml (9 fl oz/1 cup) veal or pork stock
bouquet garni
salt and freshly ground black pepper
squeeze of lemon juice

Put prunes in a bowl, pour over half the wine and leave to soak overnight.

Heat 30 g (1 oz/2 tablespoons) butter in a heavy flameproof casserole, add chops and cook quickly until browned on both sides. Remove and set aside. Add vegetables to casserole and cook, stirring occasionally, for 5-7 minutes, until lightly browned. Stir in remaining wine, bring to the boil and boil for 2-3 minutes. Add stock and bring to the boil. Return chops to casserole, add bouquet garni and salt and pepper, cover tightly and cook gently for 45 minutes.

Add prunes and soaking liquid to casserole, bring to boil, cover and cook for 30 minutes. Transfer pork and prunes to warmed serving plates and keep warm. Discard bouquet garni and boil sauce to thicken slightly. Reduce heat and gradually stir in remaining butter. Add lemon juice to taste, pour over pork and prunes and serve.

Serves 4.

PORK WITH CIDER

25 g (1 oz/2 tablespoons) butter
4 pork chops
1 onion, finely chopped
2 teaspoons Calvados or brandy
300 ml (10 fl oz/1 ¼ cups) dry cider
1 bay leaf
salt and freshly ground black pepper
2 small cooking apples, peeled, cored and sliced
1 tablespoon lemon juice
2 tablespoons crème fraîche or thick sour cream
salt and freshly ground black pepper
thyme sprigs and leaves, to garnish

Heat butter in a heavy flameproof casserole, add chops and cook quickly until browned on both sides. Remove and set aside.

Preheat oven to 180C (350F/Gas 4). Add onion to casserole and cook, stirring occasionally, for 5 minutes, until soft. Add Calvados or brandy and set alight. When flames die down, stir in cider and bring to the boil. Return chops to casserole, add bay leaf and salt and pepper, cover tightly and cook in oven for 20 minutes.

Toss apples in lemon juice. Add to casserole, cover again and cook for 10-15 minutes. Remove pork and apples from casserole with a slotted spoon, transfer to warmed serving plates and keep warm. Boil cooking liquid until lightly syrupy. Stir in crème fraîche or thick sour cream, pour over pork and apples, garnish with thyme and serve.

Serves 4.

POIS À LA FRANÇAISE

50 g (2 oz / ¼ cup) butter
3 spring onions, white parts only, finely chopped
1 small crisp lettuce, coarsely chopped
450 g (1 lb) shelled fresh or frozen peas
2 sprigs of parsley
1 ½ teaspoons chopped fresh mint
pinch of sugar (optional)
salt and freshly ground black pepper
mint sprigs, to garnish

Heat half the butter in a large saucepan, add spring onions and lettuce and cook, stirring, for 2 minutes.

Add peas, herbs, sugar, if using, and salt and pepper. Add enough water to just cover and bring to the boil. Cover and simmer gently for 12-20 minutes, depending on age of peas, until peas are tender.

Drain peas and transfer to a warmed serving dish. Stir in remaining butter, garnish with mint sprigs and serve.

Serves 4.

CAROTTES VICHY

450 g (1 lb) young carrots, thinly sliced diagonally
small pinch of bicarbonate of soda
salt
25 g (1 oz/2 tablespoons) unsalted butter
2 teaspoons sugar
1 tablespoon finely chopped fresh chervil or parsley
chervil sprigs, to garnish

Put carrots in a heavy saucepan and add enough water to just cover. Add bicarbonate of soda and a little salt.

Bring to the boil then simmer, uncovered, stirring occasionally, until carrots are tender and nearly all the water has evaporated.

Add the butter and sugar and cook, shaking pan frequently, until carrots are lightly coated with glaze. Sprinkle with chervil or parsley, garnish with chervil sprigs and serve.

Serves 4.

POTATOES FORESTIÈRE

375 g (12 oz) mixed mushrooms
450 g (1 lb) potatoes
olive oil for greasing
leaves from a bunch of parsley or basil
4 cloves garlic, crushed
salt and freshly ground black pepper
flat-leaf parsley sprigs and basil leaves, to garnish

Thinly slice mushrooms and potatoes. Preheat oven to 180C (350F/Gas 4).

Generously oil an ovenproof dish that will hold potatoes and mushrooms in a layer no more than 4 cm (1½ in) deep. In a large bowl, toss together mushrooms, potatoes, parsley or basil, garlic and salt and pepper.

Spread potato mixture into dish in an even layer and bake for about 45 minutes, until potatoes are tender, turning mixture halfway through. Leave to stand for a couple of minutes. Garnish with flat-leaf parsley and basil and serve.

Serves 4.

—GLAZED CARROTS & ONIONS—

225 g (8 oz) baby carrots
225 g (8 oz) button onions
25 g (1 oz/2 tablespoons) butter
1½ tablespoons sugar
salt and freshly ground black pepper
2 tablespoons brown veal stock or juices from roast
    meat (optional)
chopped fresh parsley, to garnish

Put carrots and onions in a heavy saucepan with half the butter, 1 tablespoon sugar and 300 ml (10 fl oz/1¼ cups) water.

Bring to the boil and simmer, uncovered, stirring occasionally, until carrots and onions are tender and water has evaporated.

Add remaining butter and sugar, salt and pepper and stock or roasting juices, if using. Increase heat slightly and cook, shaking pan occasionally, until vegetables are coated with glaze and beginning to brown. Garnish with chopped parsley and serve.

Serves 4.

— BROAD BEANS WITH SAVORY —

450 g (1 lb) shelled broad beans
few sprigs of summer savory
25 g (1 oz/2 tablespoons) butter
1 egg yolk
150 ml (5 fl oz/⅔ cup) crème fraîche or thick sour
    cream
salt and freshly ground black pepper
carrot ribbons and chervil sprigs, to garnish

Put beans and some of the savory sprigs in a saucepan of boiling salted water and cook until tender. Drain.

Heat butter in a saucepan over a low heat. Finely chop remaining savory and add to saucepan with beans.

Mix egg yolk with crème fraîche or thick sour cream. Stir into beans and cook gently, stirring, until sauce thickens: do not boil. Season with salt and pepper. Garnish with carrot ribbons and chervil sprigs and serve.

Serves 4.

– FENNEL & PARMESAN GRATIN –

4 small fennel bulbs
3 tablespoons lemon juice
50 g (2 oz/4 tablespoons) unsalted butter
1 tablespoon olive oil
50 g (2 oz) freshly grated Parmesan cheese
salt and freshly ground black pepper
25 g (1 oz/¼ cup) toasted flaked almonds

Trim feathery fronds from fennel and reserve. Cut fennel lengthways into quarters.

Add fennel and lemon juice to a saucepan of boiling salted water and cook for 15 minutes, until fennel is tender but still crisp. Drain, place on kitchen paper and drain thoroughly.

Preheat oven to 200C (400F/Gas 6). Arrange fennel in a single layer in an ovenproof dish, dot with butter, sprinkle with olive oil and cheese, season with plenty of black pepper and bake, uncovered, for 20-25 minutes, until golden. Sprinkle with almonds, garnish with reserved fennel fronds and serve.

Serves 4.

COURGETTE GRATIN

1 kg (2 lb) courgettes (zucchini), sliced
85 g (3 oz/⅓ cup) butter
450 g (1 lb) ripe tomatoes, peeled, seeded and
  chopped
2 cloves garlic, chopped
2 tablespoons chopped fresh basil or parsley
salt and freshly ground black pepper
50 g (2 oz/1 cup) fresh breadcrumbs
4-5 tablespoons finely grated Gruyère cheese
basil sprigs, to garnish

Put courgettes (zucchini) in a colander, sprinkle generously with salt and leave for 1 hour. Rinse well, drain and dry thoroughly with kitchen paper.

Preheat oven to 200C (400F/Gas 6). Heat 55 g (2 oz/¼ cup) butter in a frying pan, add courgettes (zucchini) and cook, stirring occasionally, for 7 minutes, until browned. Remove with a slotted spoon and set aside.

Add tomatoes, garlic, basil or parsley and salt and pepper to frying pan, bring to the boil and simmer gently until thickened. Stir in courgettes (zucchini). Turn into a shallow ovenproof dish. Mix together breadcrumbs and cheese and sprinkle over courgettes, (zucchini). Dot with remaining butter and bake for 25 minutes. Garnish with basil sprigs and serve.

Serves 4-6.

GRATIN SAVOYARD

1 kg (2 lb) potatoes
175 g (6 oz/1 ½ cups) grated Gruyère cheese
freshly grated nutmeg
salt and freshly ground black pepper
about 250 ml (9 fl oz/1 cup) chicken or vegetable
    stock
50 g (2 oz/¼ cup) butter, plus extra for greasing
flat-leaf parsley sprigs, to garnish

Slice potatoes very thinly, keeping them in a
bowl of cold water before slicing. Preheat
oven to 200C (400F/Gas 6).

Grease a shallow ovenproof dish with butter.
Layer potatoes in dish, sprinkling each layer
with cheese, nutmeg and salt and pepper, and
finishing with a layer of cheese.

Pour over enough stock to come almost to
the top of potatoes. Dot with butter. Bake
for 10 minutes. Lower oven temperature to
180C (350F/Gas 4) and bake for 50 minutes,
until potatoes are tender and top is golden,
and adding more stock if potatoes start to
become dry. Garnish with parsley and serve.

Serves 4.

——— GRILLED GOATS' CHEESE ———

2 tablespoons olive oil
2 tablespoons walnut or hazelnut oil
1 teaspoon black peppercorns, coarsely crushed
1 tablespoon chopped fresh thyme
4 goats' cheeses or 4 slices goats' cheese
225 g (8 oz) frisée lettuce
25 g (1 oz) rocket
4 thin slices French bread
1 tablespoon red wine vinegar
½ teaspoon Dijon mustard

Mix together oils, peppercorns and thyme. Put cheese in a small shallow dish and pour over oil mixture.

Turn cheese in oil, to coat, and leave in a cool place for 12-14 hours, turning cheese occasionally. Preheat grill. Arrange frisée and rocket on serving plates. Remove cheese from oil, reserving oil.

Brush both sides of each slice of bread with a little reserved oil. Toast one side of bread. Turn over, top with cheese and grill under a very high heat until cheese is beginning to brown. Whisk together vinegar and mustard then slowly whisk in reserved oil. Pour over salad leaves, top with the grilled goats' cheese croûtes and serve immediately.

Serves 4.

ROQUEFORT SALAD

50 g (2 oz/½ cup) walnut pieces
2 bunches watercress
115 g (4 oz) Roquefort cheese
DRESSING:
1 tablespoon red wine vinegar
½-1 teaspoon Dijon mustard
4 tablespoons olive oil
salt and freshly ground black pepper

To make dressing, whisk together vinegar and mustard then slowly pour in oil, whisking constantly. Season with salt and pepper and set aside.

Preheat grill. Spread walnut pieces on a baking sheet and grill, turning occasionally, until crisp and evenly browned.

Put watercress in a serving bowl, crumble over Roquefort cheese and sprinkle with toasted walnuts. Whisk dressing, pour over salad, toss and serve.

Serves 4.

CHICK PEA SALAD

350 g (12 oz/1 ½ cups) chick peas, soaked overnight
1 tablespoon finely chopped fresh parsley
1 ½ teaspoons finely chopped fresh tarragon
4 spring onions, finely chopped
sliced spring onion and flat-leaf parsley, to garnish
DRESSING:
2 cloves garlic, finely chopped
1 tablespoon red wine vinegar
2-3 teaspoons Dijon mustard
salt and freshly ground black pepper
4 tablespoons olive oil

Drain and rinse chick peas. Put in a saucepan
and cover with cold water.

Bring to the boil. Cover pan and simmer for
1-1½ hours, until chick peas are tender.
Meanwhile, make dressing. Mix together
garlic, vinegar, mustard and salt and pepper.
Slowly pour in the oil, whisking constantly.

Drain chick peas and immediately toss with
dressing, parsley, tarragon and spring onions.
Garnish with spring onion slices and flat-leaf
parsley and serve warm.

Serves 4.

WARM SPINACH SALAD

450 g (1 lb) young spinach leaves
6 rashers thick-cut streaky bacon, cut into strips
2 slices bread, crusts removed
4 tablespoons olive oil
4 teaspoons red wine vinegar
1 teaspoon Dijon mustard
salt and freshly ground black pepper

Put spinach in a serving bowl. Heat a non-stick frying pan, add bacon and dry-fry until crisp and brown. Remove with a slotted spoon and drain on kitchen paper.

Cut bread into cubes. Heat 1 tablespoon oil in frying pan, add bread and fry over a moderately high heat until crisp and golden. Remove and drain on kitchen paper. Add to spinach with bacon.

Stir vinegar and mustard into frying pan and bring to boil. Add remaining oil and salt and pepper. Heat through and pour over salad. Toss and serve immediately.

Serves 4.

POTATO SALAD

700 g (1 ½ lb) new potatoes
4-5 mint leaves, chopped
1 tablespoon chopped fresh chives
½ shallot, finely chopped
mint sprigs, to garnish
DRESSING:
1 tablespoon wine vinegar
2 teaspoons Dijon mustard
salt and freshly ground black pepper
3 tablespoons olive oil

Cook potatoes in a saucepan of boiling salted water for 15 minutes, until tender.

Meanwhile, make dressing. Whisk together vinegar, mustard and salt and pepper. Slowly pour in oil, whisking constantly.

Drain potatoes thoroughly, cut into halves or quarters, if necessary, then immediately toss with dressing, herbs and shallot. Leave to cool. Garnish with mint sprigs and serve.

Serves 4.

SALADE NIÇOISE

225 g (8 oz) small green beans
1 crisp lettuce
4 ripe beef tomatoes, cut into wedges
1 red pepper (capsicum), chopped
3 hard-boiled eggs, quartered
200 g (7 oz) can tuna in olive oil, drained
leaves from small bunch of flat-leaf parsley, coarsely
    chopped
16 pitted black olives
6-8 anchovy fillets, halved lengthways
DRESSING:
8 tablespoons olive oil
2 teaspoons wine vinegar
1-2 cloves garlic, crushed
salt and freshly ground black pepper

Halve beans and cook in a saucepan of boiling salted water for 10 minutes, until tender. Drain, rinse in cold water and drain again. Leave to cool. Tear lettuce leaves and arrange on a large serving plate with beans, tomatoes, pepper (capsicum), eggs and tuna.

Scatter over parsley and olives. Arrange anchovies on top in a lattice pattern. To make dressing, whisk together olive oil, vinegar, garlic and salt and pepper. Pour over salad and serve.

Serves 4.

BRAISED LENTILS

1 tablespoon olive oil
2 rashers thick-cut streaky bacon, cut into strips
1 onion, chopped
1 carrot, diced
2 cloves garlic, finely chopped
300 g (10 oz/1 ¼ cups) green or brown lentils
bouquet garni
400 g (14 oz) can chopped tomatoes
salt and freshly ground black pepper
flat-leaf parsley, to garnish

Heat oil in a large saucepan, add bacon and cook until lightly browned. Remove with a slotted spoon and drain on kitchen paper.

Add onion and carrot to pan and cook, stirring occasionally, for 7 minutes. Add garlic and cook for 2-3 minutes, until vegetables are lightly browned. Stir in lentils and mix well. Return bacon to pan and add bouquet garni. Pour in enough water to cover by 2.5 cm (1 in) and bring to the boil.

Cover and simmer for 15-25 minutes, until lentils are almost tender and most of liquid has evaporated. Add more water during cooking if necessary. Drain lentils, discarding bouquet garni, and return to pan. Add tomatoes and salt and pepper and simmer gently for 10 minutes. Garnish with flat-leaf parsley and serve.

Serves 4.

──STUFFED CABBAGE LEAVES──

1 Savoy cabbage
900 g (2 lb) chestnuts
50 g (2 oz/¼ cup) butter
115 g (4 oz) lean minced pork
1 onion, finely chopped
2 sticks celery, finely chopped
25 g (1 oz/½ cup) fresh breadcrumbs
2 eggs, lightly beaten
2½ tablespoons chopped fresh parsley
grated rind of 1 lemon
salt and freshly ground black pepper
6 slices Parma ham
basil leaves, to garnish
TOMATO & MUSHROOM SAUCE:
2 tablespoons olive oil
1 onion, finely chopped
1 clove garlic, chopped
115 g (4 oz) mushrooms, sliced
700 g (1½ lb) ripe tomatoes, peeled, seeded and
   chopped
1 tablespoon tomato purée (paste)
bouquet garni

Remove 12 large leaves from cabbage. Blanch in a saucepan of boiling water for 1 minute. Remove with a slotted spoon and drain well. Cut out central ribs. Add remaining whole cabbage to pan and cook for 4 minutes. Drain thoroughly. Cut in half, cut out core and shred leaves, discarding any thick ribs.

Cut a slit in each chestnut. Add to a saucepan of boiling water and cook for 10 minutes. Removing a few nuts from pan at a time, peel off outer and inner skins while still hot. Cook peeled chestnuts in a fresh pan of boiling water for about 20 minutes, until tender. Drain and coarsely chop.

Heat butter in a large frying pan, add shredded cabbage and cook, stirring occasionally, for 7-8 minutes, until tender. Remove with a slotted spoon and transfer to a large bowl. Add pork, onion and celery to pan and cook, stirring occasionally, until pork is browned. Add to cabbage with chestnuts, breadcrumbs, eggs, parsley, lemon rind and salt and pepper.

Line a small bowl with a piece of muslin. Put two blanched cabbage leaves into bowl then cover with a slice of ham. Add one-sixth of stuffing. Gather up ends of cloth and tie with string to make a tight ball. Repeat with remaining ingredients to make six balls. Add to a large pan of boiling water, weight down with a plate and simmer for 30 minutes.

Meanwhile, make tomato and mushroom sauce. Heat oil in a saucepan, add onion and cook for 2-3 minutes. Stir in garlic, mushrooms, tomatoes, tomato purée (paste), bouquet garni and salt and pepper. Simmer for 10 minutes, until thickened. Discard bouquet garni. Lift cabbage parcels from pan, drain well, then unwrap and turn out onto warmed serving plates. Pour over sauce, garnish with basil leaves and serve.

Serves 6.

RATATOUILLE

2 aubergines (eggplant), sliced
3 courgettes (zucchini), sliced
3-4 tablespoons olive oil
1 Spanish onion, very thinly sliced
3 cloves garlic, crushed
2 large red peppers (capsicum), thinly sliced
4 ripe beef tomatoes, peeled, seeded and chopped
leaves from a few sprigs of thyme, marjoram and
　　oregano
salt and freshly ground black pepper
2 tablespoons each chopped fresh parsley and basil

Put aubergine (eggplant) and courgette (zucchini) in a colander, sprinkle generously with salt and leave for 1 hour.

Rinse well, drain and dry thoroughly with kitchen paper. Heat 2 tablespoons oil in a heavy flameproof casserole, add aubergine (eggplant) and cook, stirring occasionally, for a few minutes. Add 1 tablespoon oil, the onions and garlic and cook, stirring occasionally, for 2-3 minutes. Add peppers (capsicum) and cook, stirring occasionally, for 1-2 minutes.

Add courgettes (zucchini) to casserole with more oil if necessary. Cook, stirring occasionally, for 2-3 minutes, then add tomatoes, thyme, marjoram and oregano. Season lightly with salt and pepper, cover and cook very gently for 30-40 minutes, stirring occasionally. Stir in parsley and basil and cook, uncovered, for 5-10 minutes, until liquid has evaporated. Serve warm or cold.

Serves 4.

CLAFOUTIS

700 g (1 ½ lb) ripe cherries, pitted
3 eggs
few drops of almond essence
3 tablespoons caster sugar, plus extra for sprinkling
3 tablespoons plain flour
450 ml (16 fl oz/2 cups) milk
25 g (1 oz/2 tablespoons) butter, plus extra for
   greasing
mint sprigs, to decorate

Preheat oven to 220C (425F/Gas 7). Grease a large shallow ovenproof dish with butter and add the cherries.

Mix together eggs, almond essence, sugar and flour. Put milk into a saucepan, bring almost to the boil and stir into egg mixture.

Pour over cherries, dot with butter and bake for 20-25 minutes, until just set and lightly browned. Cut into squares, sprinkle with sugar, decorate with mint and serve warm.

Serves 4.

COEURS À LA CRÈME

450 ml (16 fl oz/2 cups) fromage frais or curd cheese
250 ml (9 fl oz/1 cup) double (thick) cream
3 egg whites
TO SERVE:
sugar or vanilla sugar
fresh fruit

Line six individual coeurs à la crème moulds with pieces of muslin.

In a large bowl, beat fromage frais or curd cheese until smooth then whisk in cream. Whisk egg whites until stiff. Fold into the cheese mixture. Spoon into moulds, put moulds in a roasting tin or on a tray and leave in the refrigerator for 12-24 hours, to drain: the longer the mixture is left, the firmer it becomes.

Turn moulds onto chilled serving plates. Decorate with mint sprigs and serve with sugar or vanilla sugar and fresh fruit.

Serves 6.

Note: To make vanilla sugar, simply store a vanilla pod in a jar of sugar, so that it absorbs the flavour.

CRÈME CARAMEL

550 ml (20 fl oz/2 ½ cups) milk
1 vanilla pod
2 eggs
2 egg yolks
75 g (3 oz/⅓ cup) sugar
mint sprigs, to decorate
CARAMEL:
115 g (4 oz/½ cup) caster sugar

To make caramel, put caster sugar in a small heavy saucepan with 5 tablespoons water and heat gently until sugar has dissolved. Increase heat and boil until golden brown.

Remove from heat and pour into six 150 ml (5 fl oz/⅔ cup) ramekins, turning dishes to coat sides with caramel. Put in a roasting tin and leave to cool. Preheat oven to 160C (325F/Gas 3). Put milk and vanilla pod into a small saucepan and bring to the boil. Cover, remove from the heat and leave to infuse for 20 minutes. Put eggs, egg yolks and sugar in a large bowl and whisk together. Remove vanilla pod from milk and return milk to the boil. Stir into egg mixture.

Strain into ramekins. Pour boiling water into roasting tin to come halfway up sides of ramekins and bake for 40-50 minutes, until lightly set. Remove from tin and leave to cool. One hour before serving, run knife around edge of caramels and turn out onto serving plates. Decorate with mint and serve.

Serves 6.

—PETITS POTS AU CHOCOLAT—

550 ml (20 fl oz/2½ cups) single (light) cream or milk
1 vanilla pod
butter for greasing
1 egg
5 egg yolks
3 tablespoons caster sugar
225 g (8 oz) plain chocolate, chopped
1 tablespoon instant coffee granules
whipped cream and chocolate shavings, to decorate

Put cream or milk and vanilla pod into a small saucepan and bring to the boil over a low heat. Cover, remove from heat and leave to infuse for 15 minutes.

Preheat oven to 150C (300F/Gas 2). Butter individual custard pots or ramekins and put in a roasting tin. Put egg, egg yolks and sugar in a large bowl and whisk together until thick and pale. Remove vanilla pod from cream or milk and return to the boil.

Remove milk from heat, add chocolate and coffee and stir until dissolved. Stir into egg mixture. Strain into pots. Pour boiling water into roasting tin to come halfway up sides of pots and bake for about 1 hour, until very lightly set. Transfer pots to a wire rack and leave to cool. Chill. Decorate with whipped cream and chocolate shavings and serve.

Serves 6-8.

———— OEUFS À LA NEIGE ————

3 eggs, separated
115 g (4 oz/½ cup) caster sugar
2 egg yolks
450 ml (16 fl oz/2 cups) milk
1½-2 tablespoons Cointreau or orange flower water
    or rose water
strips of orange rind and mint sprigs, to decorate

Whisk egg whites until stiff but not dry. Gradually whisk in half the sugar until mixture is stiff and shiny. Meanwhile, bring a large frying pan of water to the boil.

Lower heat beneath pan so water is barely simmering. Float dessertspoonfuls of egg white onto water, a few at a time so they are not crowded, and poach for 2-3 minutes, turning halfway through. Remove with a slotted spoon, transfer to a tilted tray and leave to drain. Whisk all 5 egg yolks with remaining sugar until thick and pale. Put milk into a saucepan and bring to the boil.

Stir a little milk into egg yolk mixture then, over a low heat, stir back into milk. Cook gently, stirring, until thickened slightly: do not boil. Leave to cool, stirring occasionally. Just before serving, add Cointreau or flower water and pour custard into shallow serving bowls. Float meringues on top, decorate with orange rind and mint sprigs and serve.

Serves 4-6.

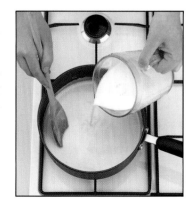

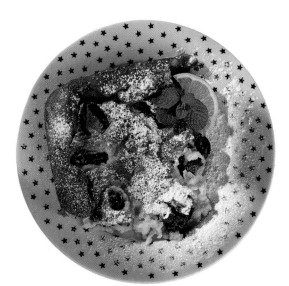

—— BRETON PRUNE PUDDING ——

200 g (7 oz/1 ⅓ cups) ready-to-eat prunes
4 tablespoons rum or hot water
25 g (1 oz/2 tablespoons) butter
50 g (2 oz/½ cup) plain flour
about 3 tablespoons sugar
4 eggs, beaten
450 ml (16 fl oz/2 cups) milk
icing sugar, for dusting
lemon wedges and mint sprigs, to decorate

Put prunes in a bowl, add rum or hot water and leave for 2 hours. Put butter in a shallow ovenproof dish and put in oven while preheating it to 200C (400F/Gas 6).

Combine flour and sugar in a bowl. Gradually stir in eggs and then milk, to make a smooth batter. Drain liquid from prunes and add liquid to batter.

Put prunes into ovenproof dish, carefully pour over batter and bake for about 1 hour, until well risen, just set in centre and golden brown on top. Leave to cool slightly. Cut into squares and dust with icing sugar. Decorate with lemon wedges and mint sprigs and serve warm.

Serves 4.

PEARS IN RED WINE

4 firm Williams or Comice pears, peeled,
  with stalks left on
4 cloves
8 prunes
550 ml (20 fl oz/2 ½ cups) red wine
1-2 tablespoons sugar
1 ½ cinnamon sticks
1 vanilla pod
2 tablespoons crème de cassis
orange slices and bay leaves, to decorate

Preheat oven to lowest setting. Stud pears
with cloves and put into a large heavy
casserole with prunes.

Put wine, sugar, cinnamon sticks and vanilla
into a saucepan and bring to the boil over a
low heat, stirring until sugar has dissolved.
Pour over pears, cover and bake for 3 hours,
turning and basting pears twice.

Transfer pears and prunes to a dish, standing
pears upright. Remove vanilla pod. Add
cassis to cooking liquid and boil rapidly until
lightly syrupy. Pour sauce over pears and
leave to cool. Chill before serving. Slice pears
and arrange on serving plates. Decorate with
orange slices and bay leaves and serve.

Serves 4.

──── PEACHES IN WHITE WINE ────

4 ripe peaches
4 raspberries, strawberries or small pieces of
　almond paste
1-2 tablespoons icing or caster sugar, preferably
　vanilla flavoured
300 ml (10 fl oz/1 ¼ cups) fruity white wine, chilled
lemon twists, raspberries and raspberry leaves, to
　decorate

Put peaches in a large bowl, cover with boiling water and leave for about 20 seconds. Remove peaches from water, peel, then cut in half and remove stones.

Put a raspberry, strawberry or piece of almond paste in cavity of each peach and reassemble peaches. Put peaches in four serving dishes, sprinkle with sugar and pour over wine. Cover and chill, turning peaches once. Decorate and serve.

Serves 4.

——SUMMER FRUIT GRATIN——

2 large peaches, peeled and sliced
50 g (2 oz) raspberries
115 g (4 oz) strawberries, sliced
50 g (2 oz) redcurrants and blueberries or
   blackcurrants
2 tablespoons kirsch or Cointreau (optional)
2 tablespoons caster sugar
300 ml (10 fl oz/1 ¼ cups) crème fraîche or double
   (thick) cream
85-115 g (3-4 oz) soft brown sugar

Divide the fruit between four heatproof serving dishes. Sprinkle with kirsch or Cointreau, if using, and caster sugar.

Whip crème fraîche or cream until it forms soft peaks. Spread over fruit and chill for at least 1 hour.

Preheat grill to very hot. Sprinkle a thick even layer of brown sugar over crème fraîche or cream. Grill until sugar is bubbling and caramelized. Serve immediately.

Serves 4.

TARTE AU CITRON

3 eggs
1 egg yolk
150 g (5 oz/¾ cup) caster sugar
grated rind and juice of 3 lemons
grated rind and juice of 1 orange
70 g (2½ oz/½ cup) icing sugar
thinly pared rind of 1 lemon
icing sugar for dusting
lemon twists and chervil sprigs, to decorate
PÂTE SUCRÉE:
200 g (7 oz/¾ cup) plain flour
pinch of salt
4 tablespoons caster sugar
115 g (4 oz/½ cup) unsalted butter, softened
2 egg yolks

To make pâte sucrée, sift flour and salt onto a marble slab or a work surface and make a well in centre. Put sugar, butter and egg yolks into well and pinch them together to form a paste, then lightly draw in the flour, adding about 1 tablespoon cold water to make a soft but firm dough. Cover and chill for 2 hours.

Roll out pastry on a lightly floured surface and line a 23.5 cm (9½ in) loose-bottomed fluted flan tin, pressing pastry well into sides and base. Run rolling pin over top of tin to cut off excess pastry. Chill for 20 minutes. Preheat oven to 200C (400F/Gas 6).

Prick base of pastry case with a fork, line with greaseproof paper or foil and fill with baking beans. Put flan tin on a baking sheet and bake for 10-12 minutes. Lower oven temperature to 190C (375F/Gas 5). Remove paper and beans and bake for 5 minutes, until golden. Transfer tin to a wire rack and leave to cool. Leave oven on.

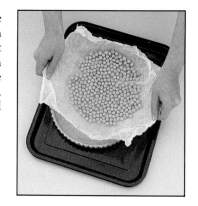

Mix together eggs, egg yolk, caster sugar and lemon and orange rind and juice. Return flan tin to baking sheet and ladle in filling. Bake for 25-30 minutes, until set. Transfer tin to a wire rack, cool slightly, then remove outer ring of flan tin. Leave tart to cool completely.

Put icing sugar and 150 ml (5 fl oz/⅔ cup) water in a small pan and heat gently, stirring, until dissolved. Boil for 2 minutes then add pared lemon rind and simmer until glassy. Remove with a slotted spoon and leave to cool on greaseproof paper. Just before serving, dust tart thickly with sifted icing sugar and scatter over candied lemon rind. Garnish with lemon twists and chervil sprigs and serve with cream, if liked.

Serves 6-8.

TARTE TATIN

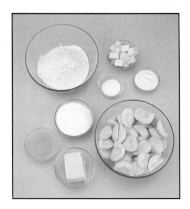

115 g (4 oz/½ cup) unsalted butter, softened
115 g (4 oz/½ cup) caster sugar
about 1.3 kg (3 lb) firm, well-flavoured apples, such
  as Cox's, peeled, cored and cut into wedges
juice of 1 lemon
strips of lemon rind and mint sprigs, to decorate
PASTRY:
225 g (8 oz/2 cups) plain flour
1 tablespoon caster sugar
130 g (4½ oz/½ cup) butter, diced
2-3 tablespoons crème fraîche

To make pastry, combine flour and sugar in a
bowl. Add butter and rub in until mixture
resembles fine breadcrumbs. Add enough
crème fraîche to bind to a dough. Form into
a ball, cover and chill for at least 30 minutes.

Spread butter over base of a heavy 23.5 cm
(9½ in) cake tin or ovenproof frying pan.
Sprinkle over sugar and arrange apples on
top, rounded-side down.

Sprinkle with lemon juice and cook over a moderately high heat, shaking tin or pan occasionally, for 20-30 minutes, until apples are lightly caramelized. If a lot of juice is produced, pour it off into a saucepan, boil to a thick syrup and pour back over apples.

Preheat oven to 220C (425F/Gas 7). Roll out pastry on a lightly floured surface until slightly larger than tin or pan. Lay pastry on top of apples, tucking edge of pastry down side of tin or pan.

Prick pastry lightly with a fork and put tin or pan on a baking sheet. Bake for 20 minutes, until pastry is golden. Turn tart onto a warmed serving plate, decorate with lemon rind and mint sprigs and serve with cream.

Serves 6-8.

Note: Be careful when turning out the tart as the syrup will be very hot and can burn.

RED FRUIT TART

23.5 cm (9 ½ in) loose-bottomed fluted flan tin lined
  with pâte sucrée (see page 114)
about 26 each raspberries, halved strawberries and
  pitted cherries
3 tablespoons red fruit jam
1 tablespoon lemon juice
raspberries and raspberry leaves, to decorate
CRÈME PÂTISSIÈRE:
150 ml (5 fl oz/⅔ cup) milk
150 ml (5 fl oz/⅔ cup) single (light) cream
1 vanilla pod
3 egg yolks
50 g (2 oz/¼ cup) sugar
1 tablespoon plain flour
1 ½ tablespoons cornflour
15 g (½ oz/1 tablespoon) unsalted butter

To make crème pâtissière, put milk, cream
and vanilla pod in a saucepan and heat gently
to simmering point. Remove from heat,
cover and leave for 30 minutes. Whisk egg
yolks and sugar until pale and very thick. Stir
in flour and cornflour. Remove vanilla pod
from milk and return to the boil. Slowly
pour into egg mixture, whisking constantly.
Return to pan and bring to boil, whisking.
Simmer for 2-3 minutes. Remove from heat,
stir in butter and pour into a bowl. Leave to
cool, stirring occasionally. Cover and chill.
Preheat oven to 200C (400F/Gas 6).

Prick pastry case with a fork, line with
greaseproof paper or foil and fill with baking
beans. Bake for 10-12 minutes. Lower oven
temperature to 190C (375F/Gas 5). Remove
paper and beans and bake for 8-10 minutes.
Cool on a wire rack. Fill pastry case with
crème patissière and arrange fruit on top. Put
jam and lemon juice in a pan and heat gently,
to soften. Pass through a sieve and brush
over fruit. Leave to cool, decorate and serve.

Serves 6.

MADELEINES

3 eggs, separated
115 g (4 oz/ ½ cup) caster sugar
115 g (4 oz/1 cup) plain flour, plus extra for dusting
1 teaspoon baking powder
150 g (4 oz/ ½ cup) unsalted butter, melted, plus
    extra for greasing
1 ½ tablespoons lemon juice
grated rind of 1 large lemon
icing sugar for dusting
strips of lemon rind, chervil sprigs and fresh fruit,
    to decorate

Whisk together egg yolks and caster sugar until thick and pale yellow. Sift flour and baking powder into mixture.

Using a large metal spoon, fold in flour and baking powder, slowly pouring in butter and lemon juice at same time. Whisk egg whites until stiff but not dry. Fold egg whites and lemon rind into egg yolk mixture. Cover and chill for 30 minutes. Preheat oven to 220C (425F/Gas 7). Generously grease madeleine moulds with butter and dust with flour.

Spoon mixture into moulds so they are no more than two-thirds full. Bake in the oven for 7 minutes, until risen. Lower oven temperature to 190C (375F/Gas 5) and bake for a further 7 minutes, until pale gold on top and slightly darker around edges. Remove from moulds, transfer to a wire rack and dust with icing sugar. Decorate and serve warm.

Makes 20.

Note: The madeleines can be baked in batches, if necessary.

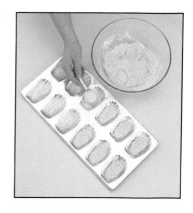

INDEX